TO THE SEA

Salt sticky hair, ice cream smiles, sandcastles and sun-speckled freckles. Small boats, overfishing, plastic pollution and rising sea levels.

As climate change imposes more circumstantial realities on us, the sea becomes ever more important in our everyday lives.

We reminisce on childhood holidays and collecting seashells, dog walks on the beach, and the soothing sound of gently lapping waves.

But we must remember, although it's bigger than all of us, vast and powerful, the sea very much needs us to look after it.

Here, within these pages, photographers share their visions of the sea – environmental, actual, emotional, and more.

The Dry S3 2025

Dom,

It has been a total joy & a privilege getting to know you & work with you over the past four years.

You have created an icon in Bernie & she will be missed ... until the Christmas Special!

Grá mór,

Siobhán

x

100 IMAGES

AN ODE TO THE OCEAN
SOMETHING FOR THE SEA

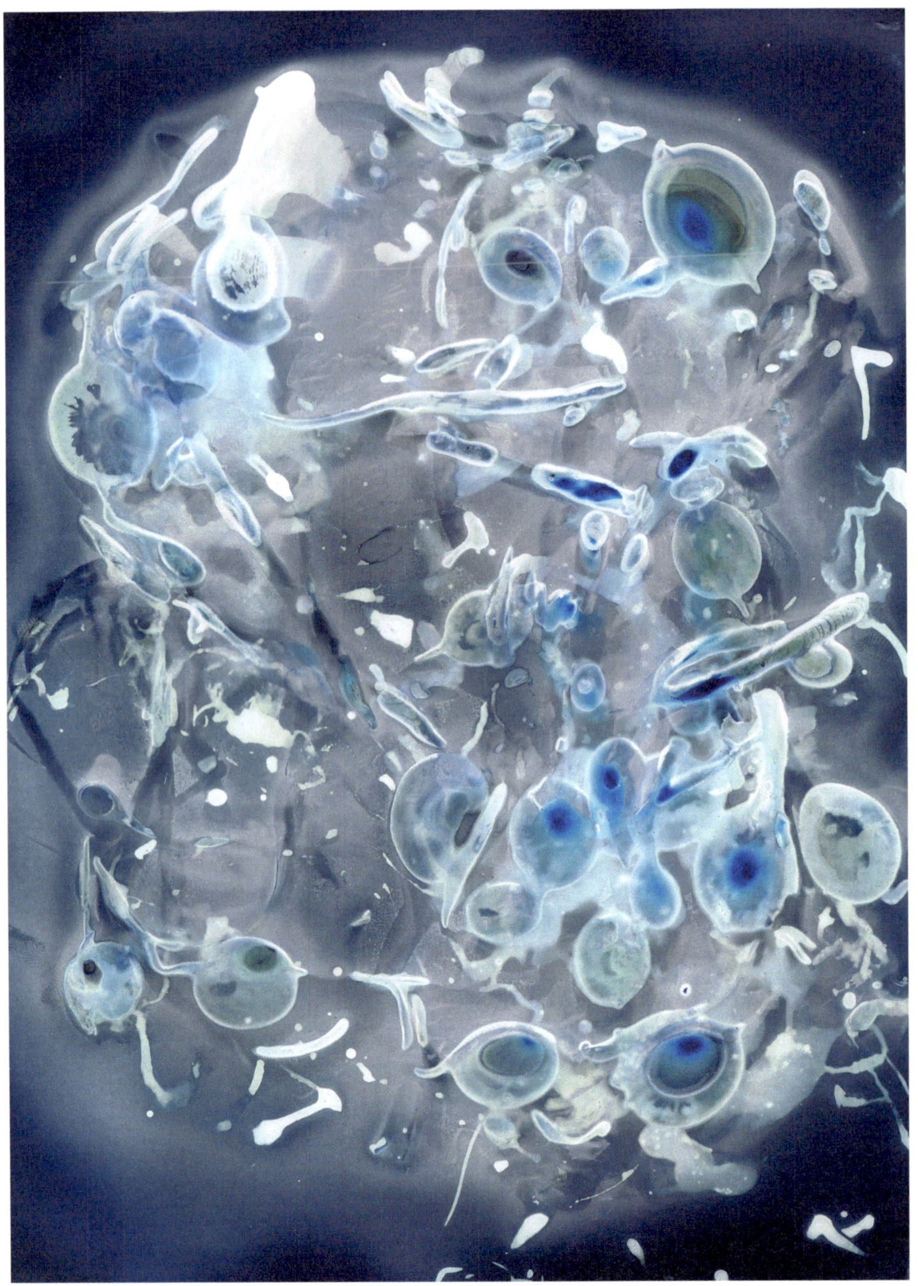

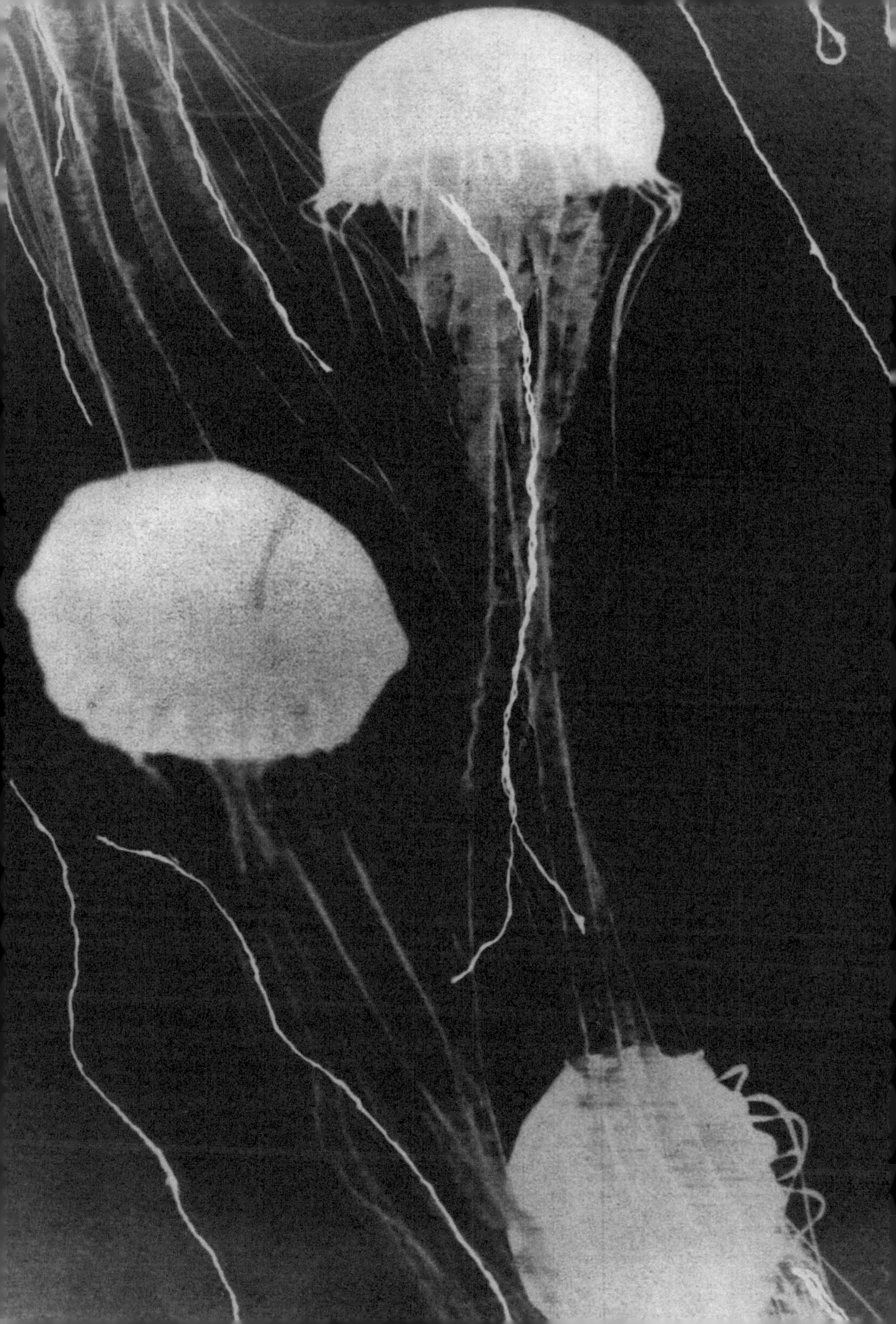

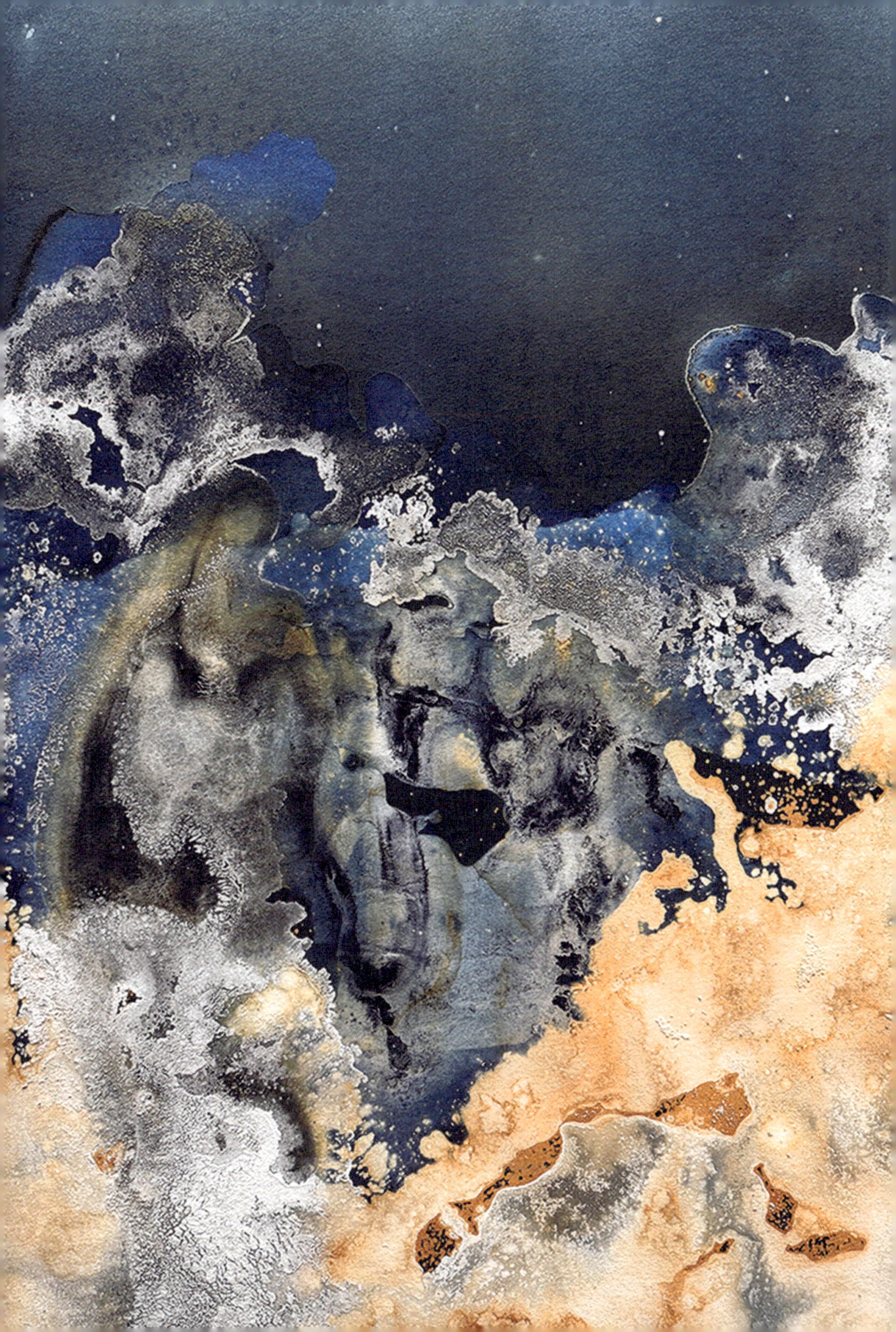

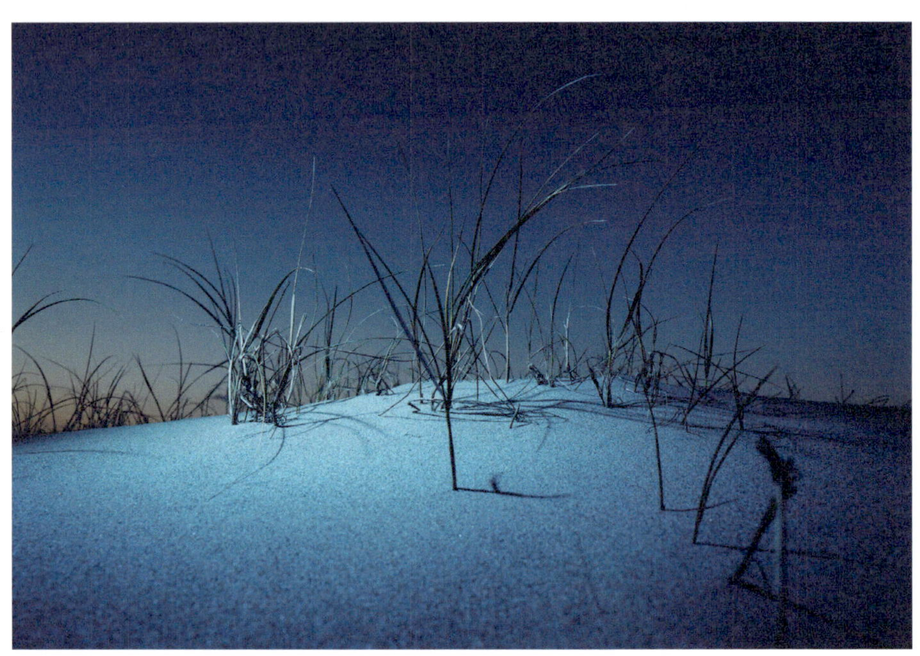

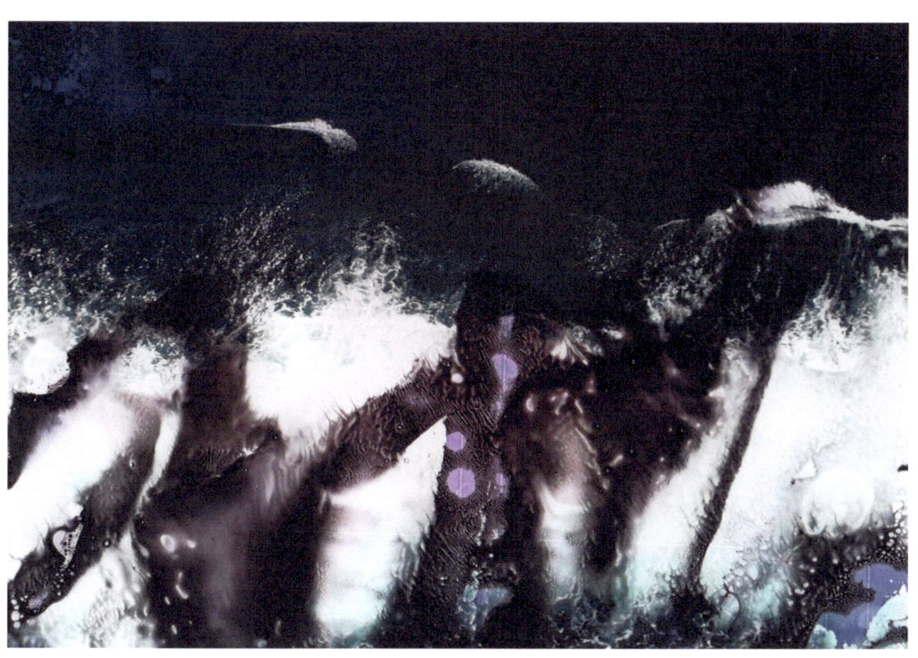

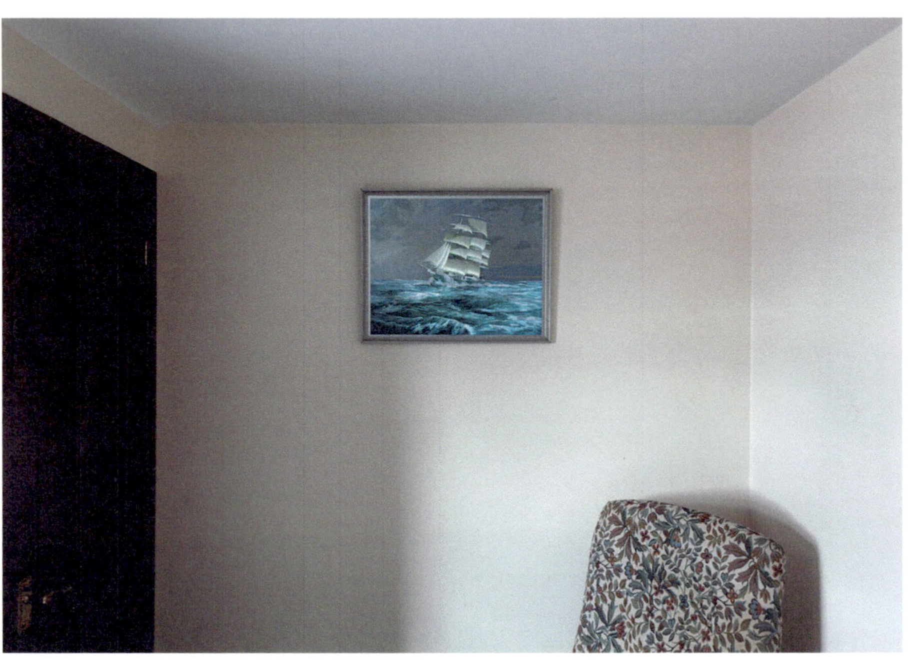

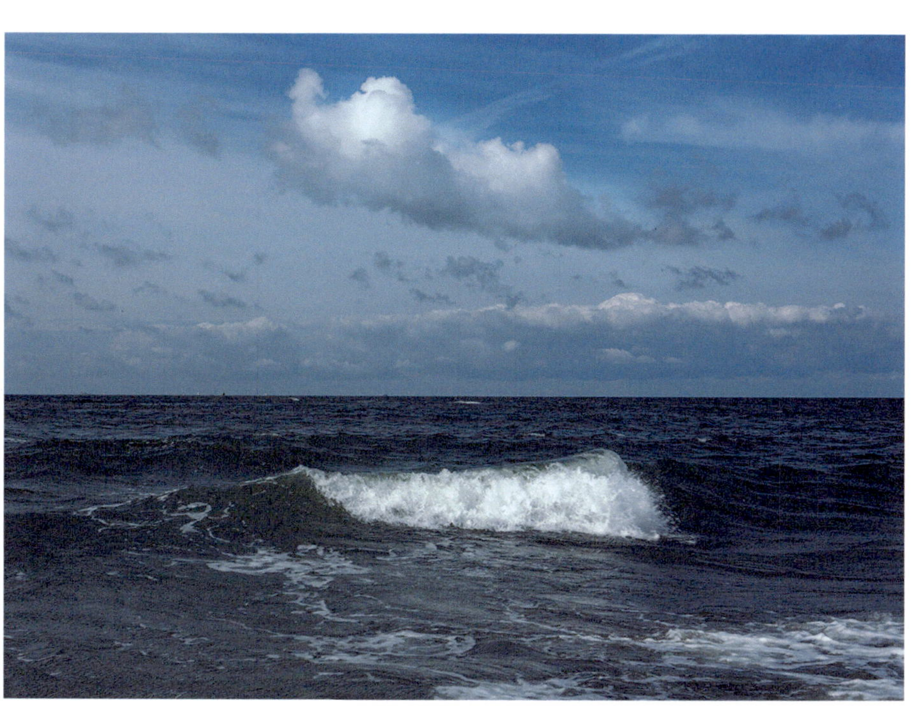

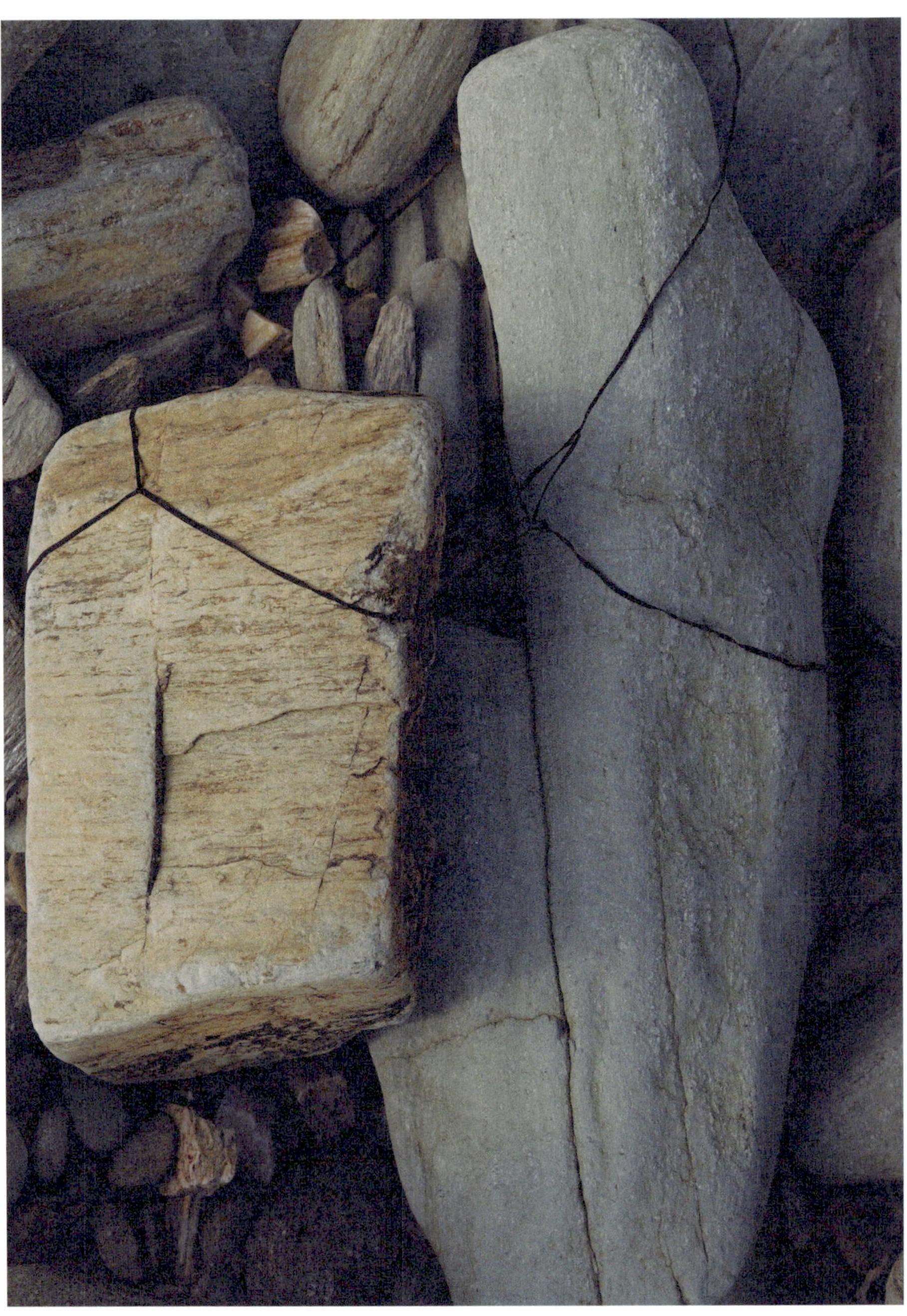

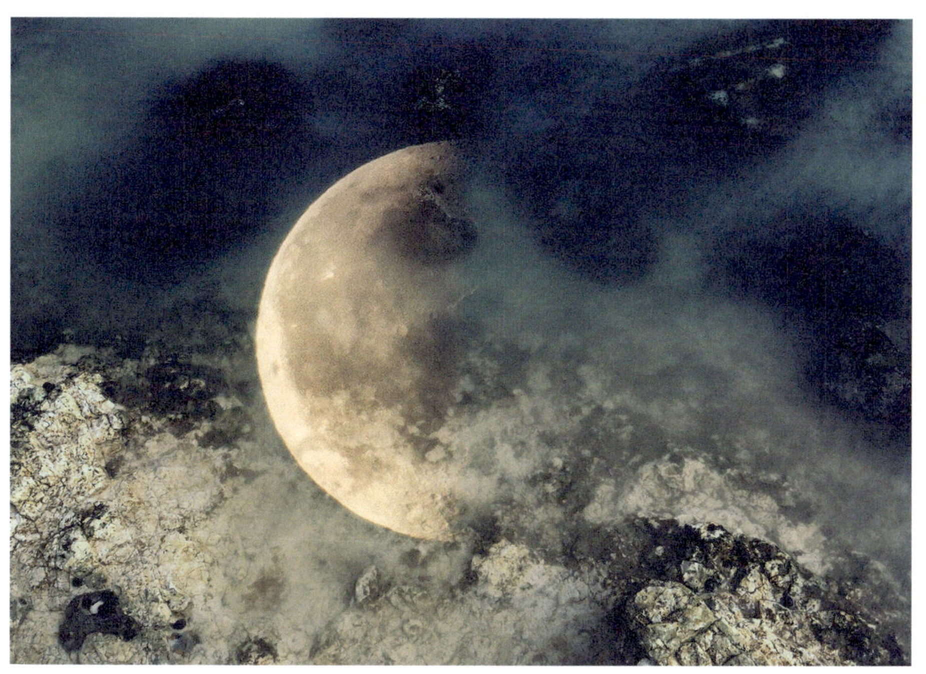

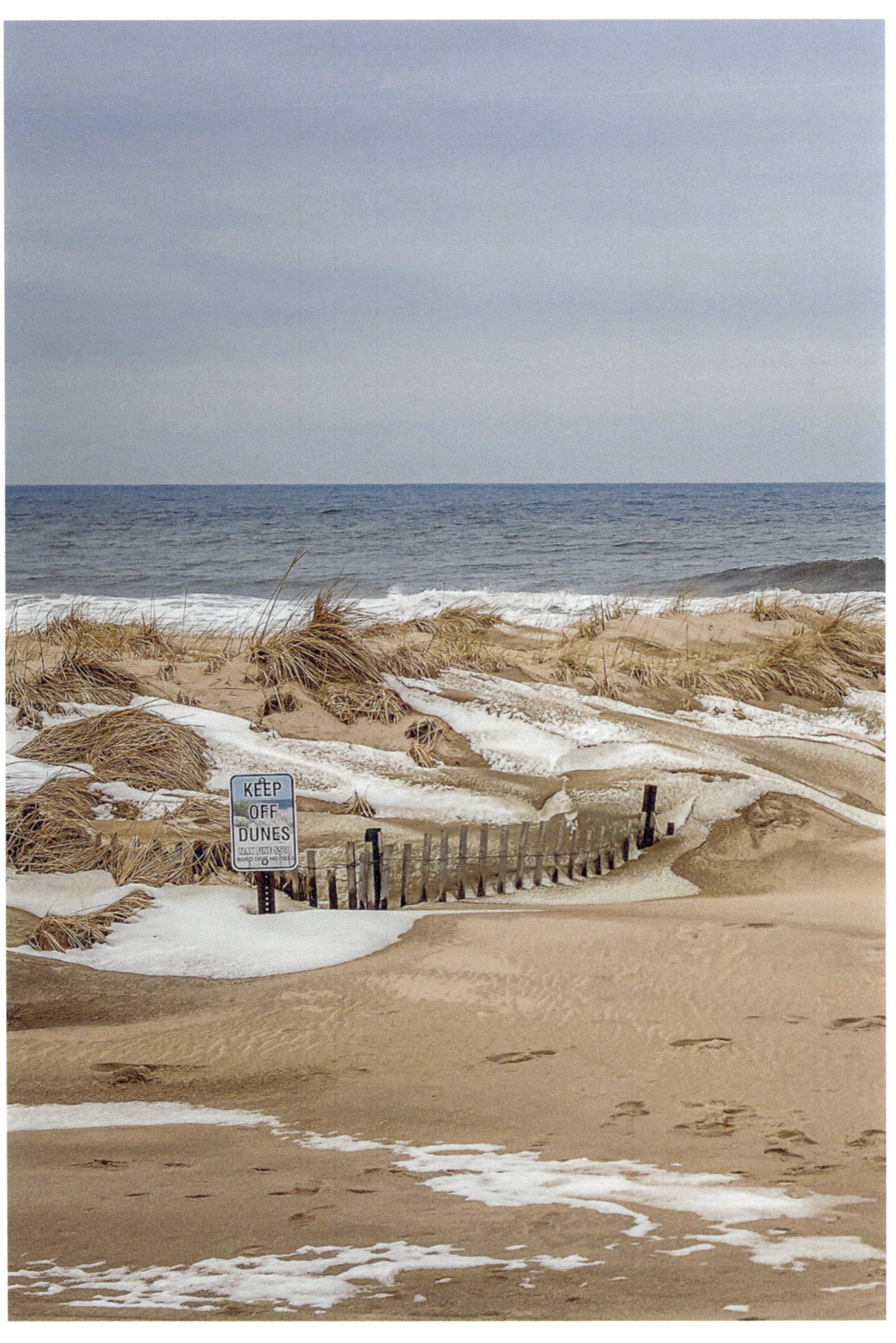
KEEP
OFF
DUNES
MAX FINE $500

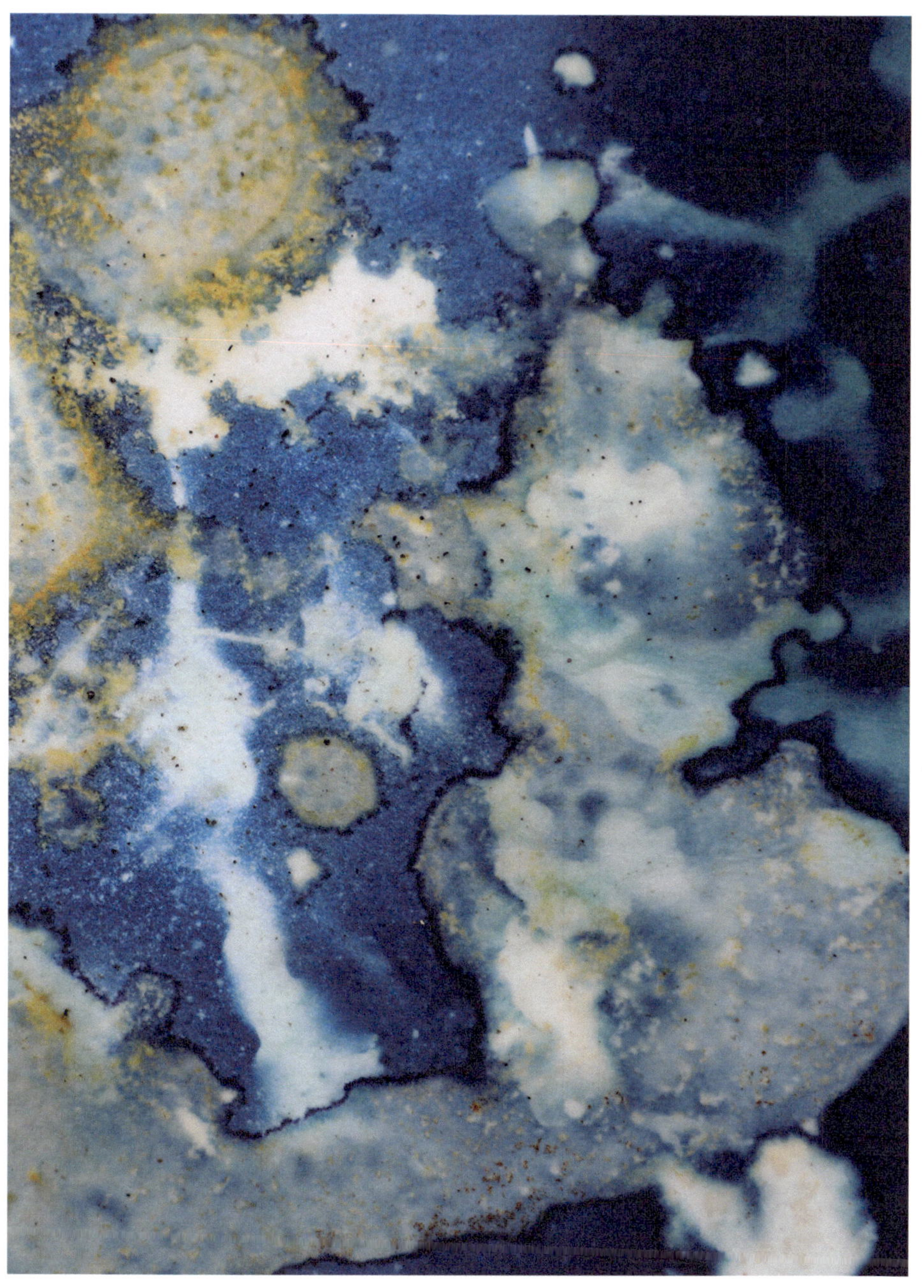

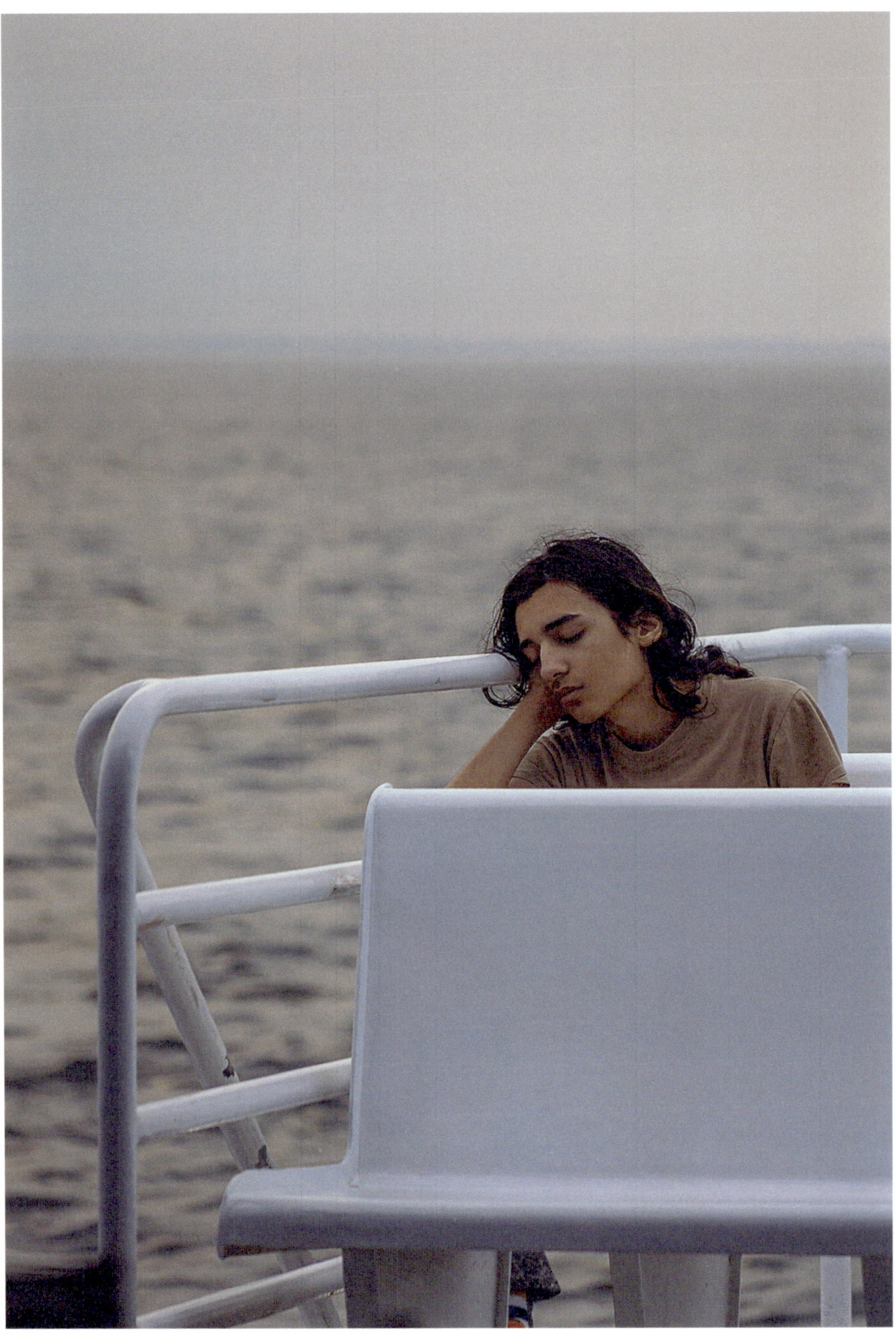

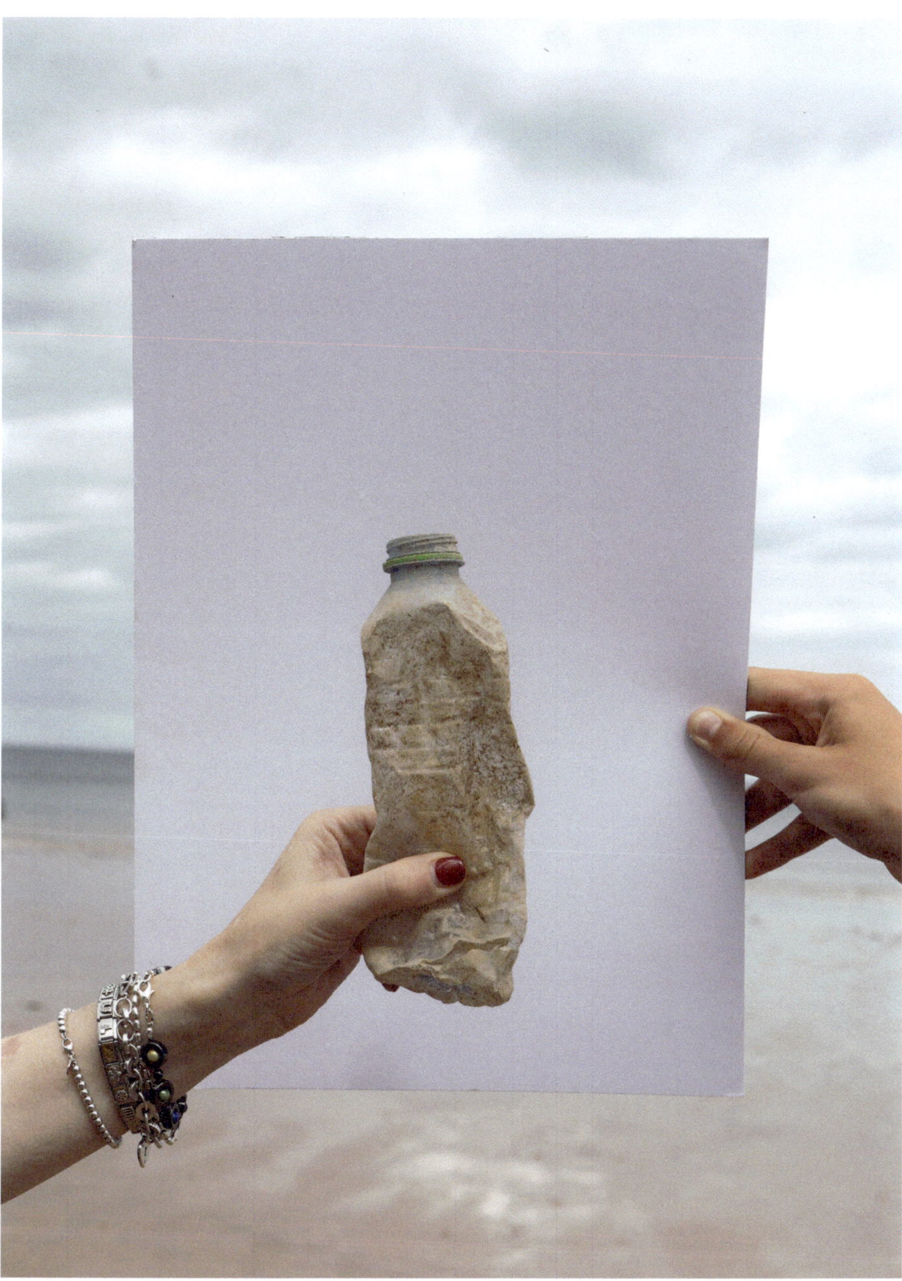

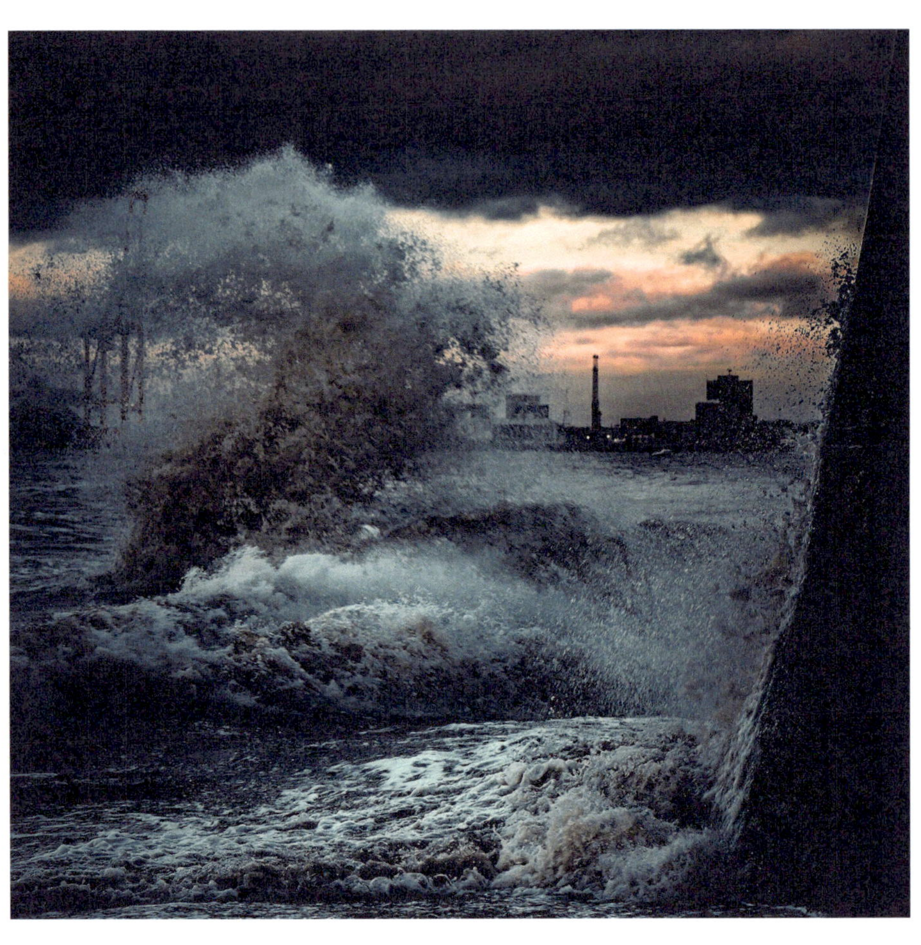

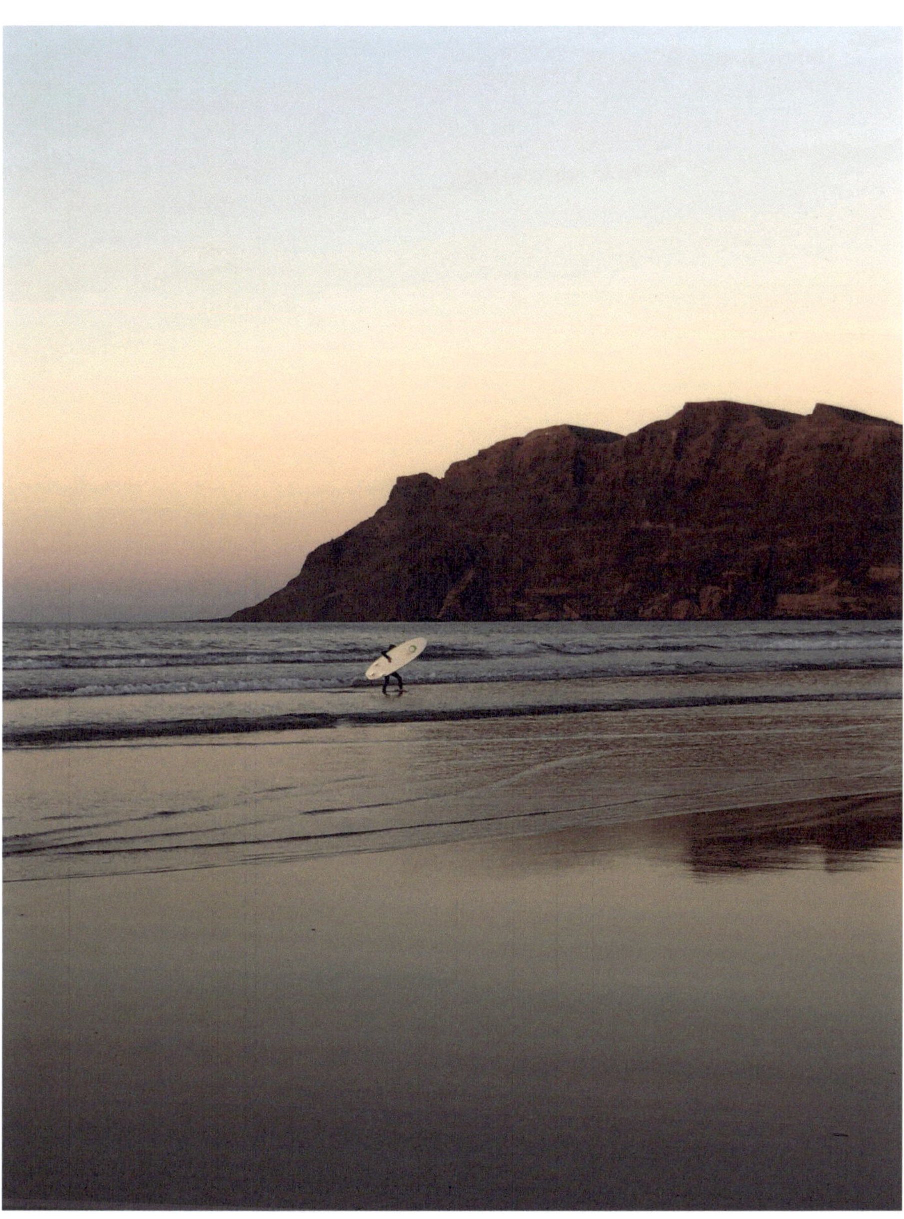

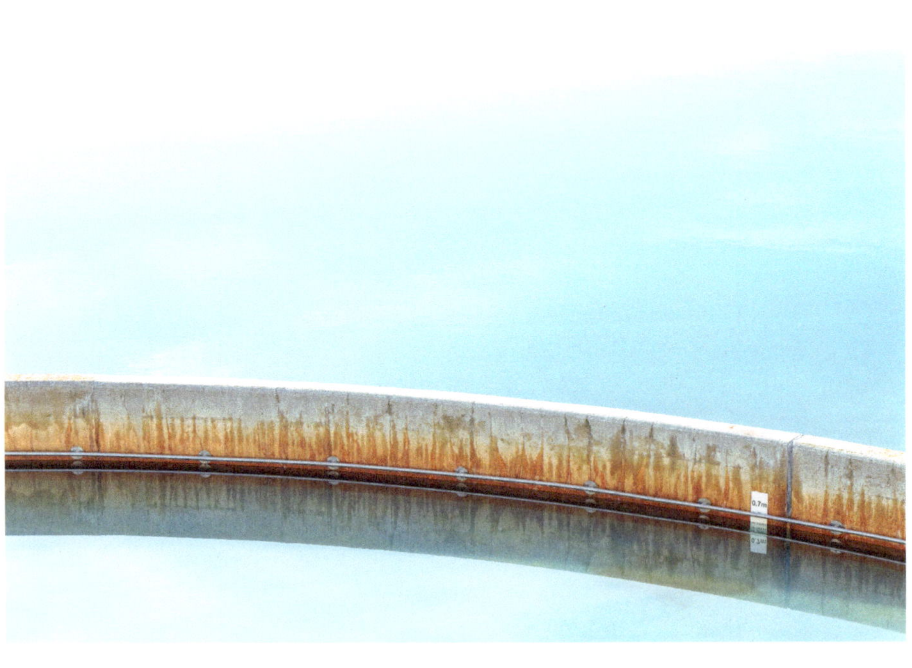
0.7m

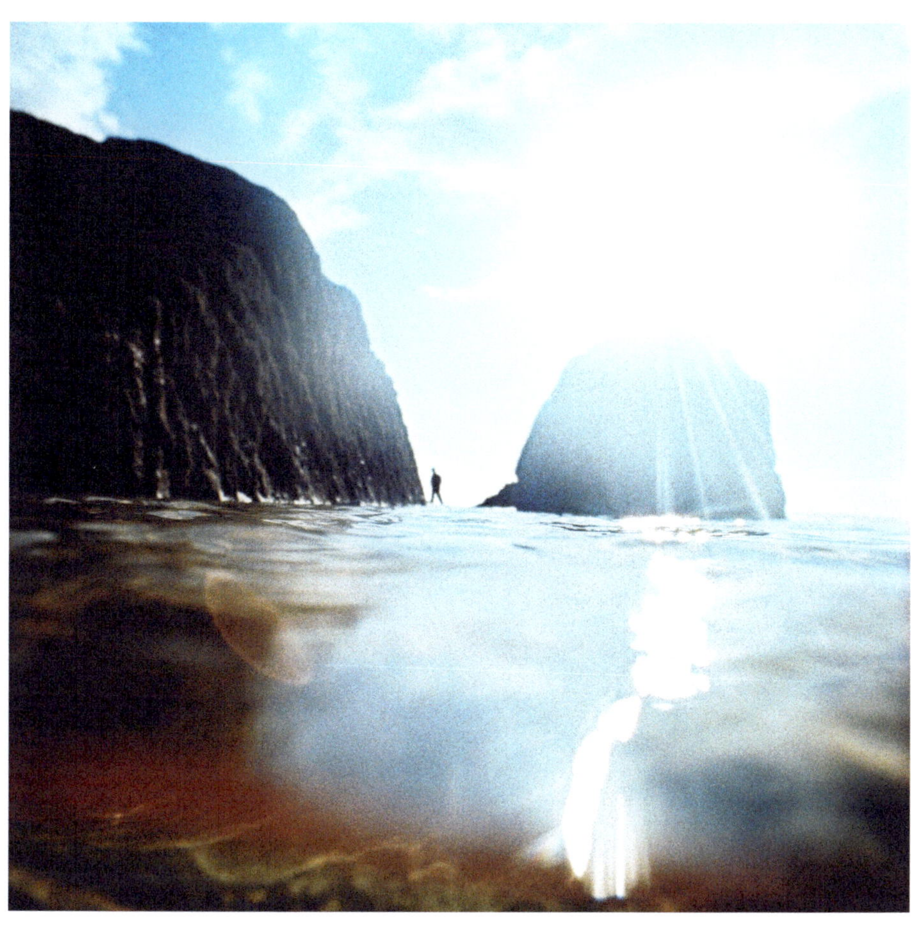

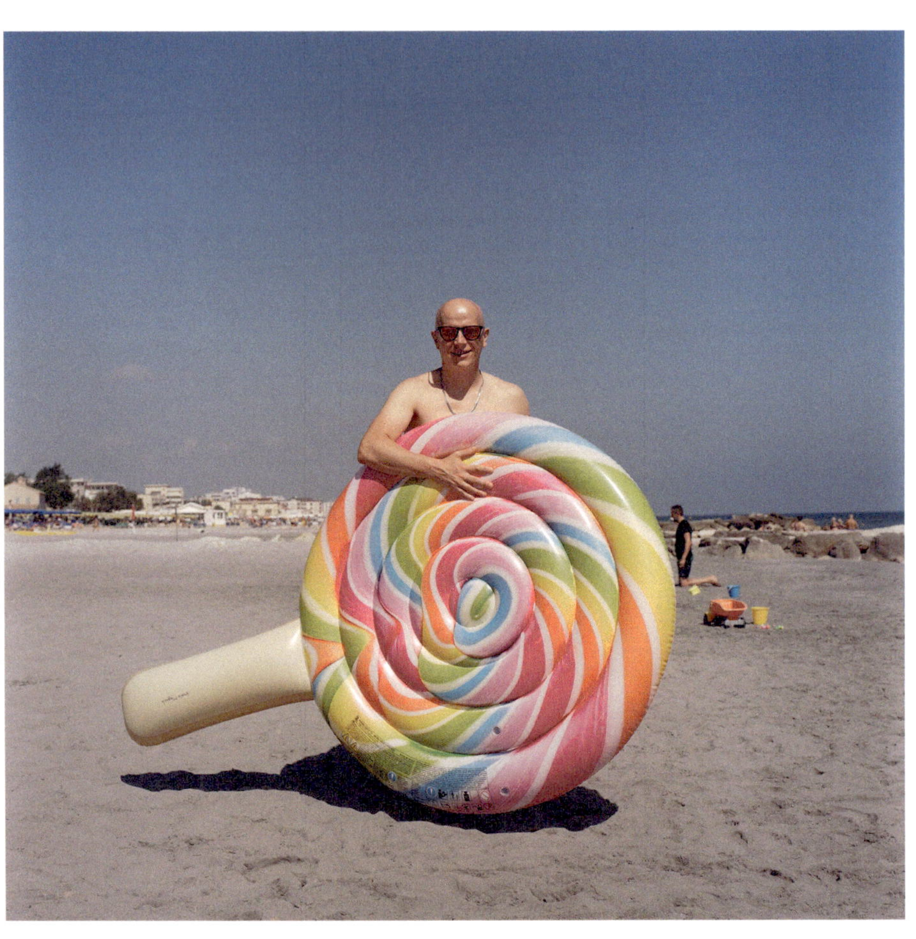

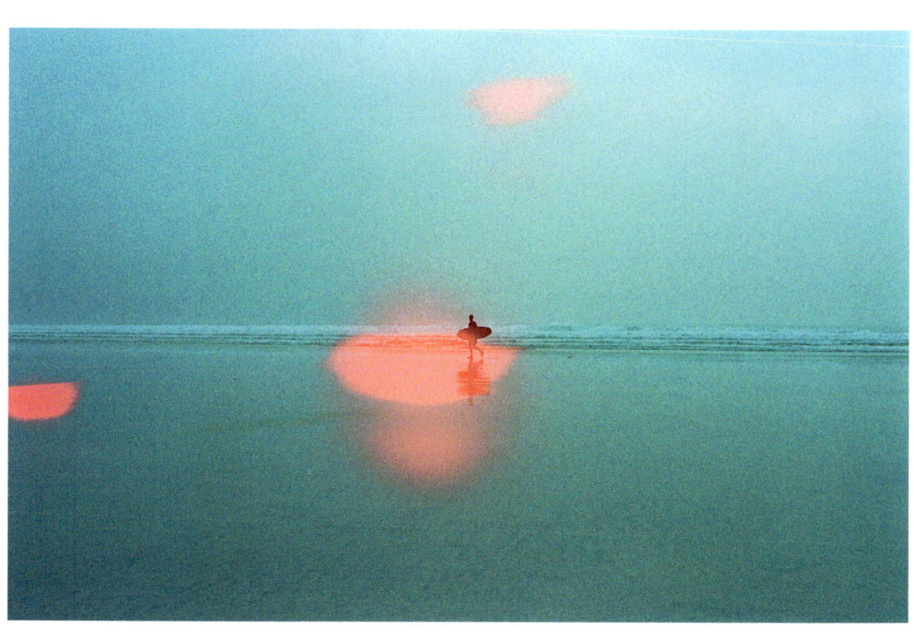

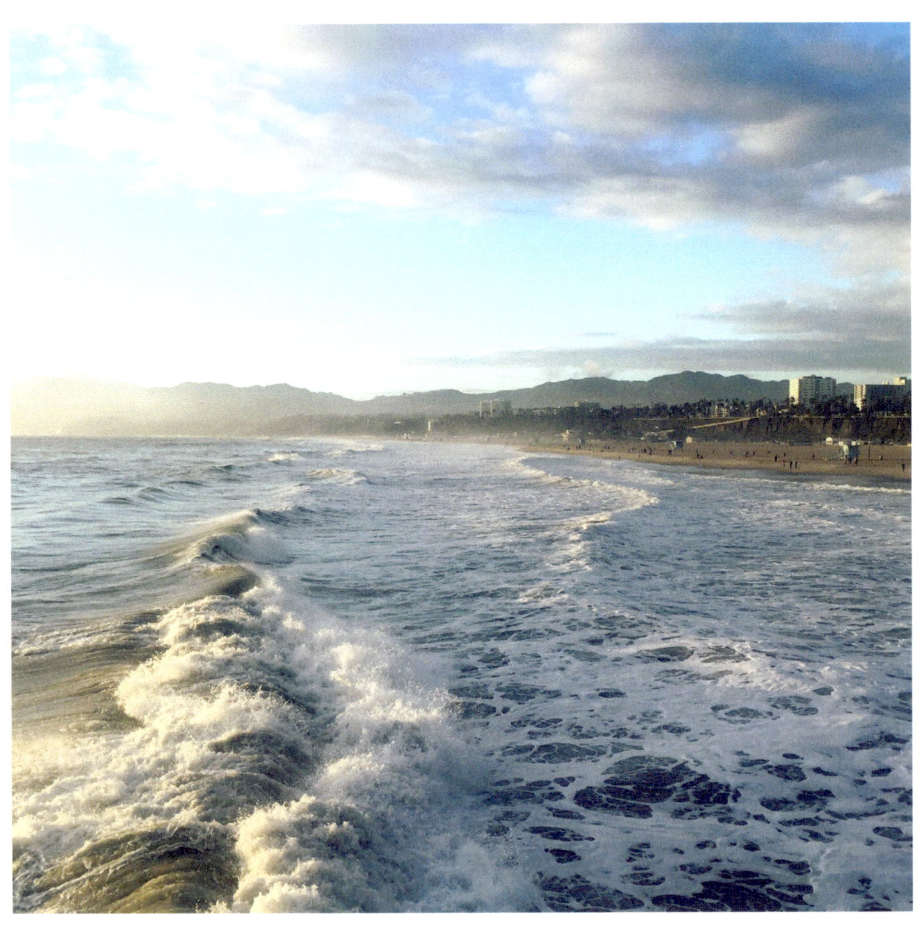

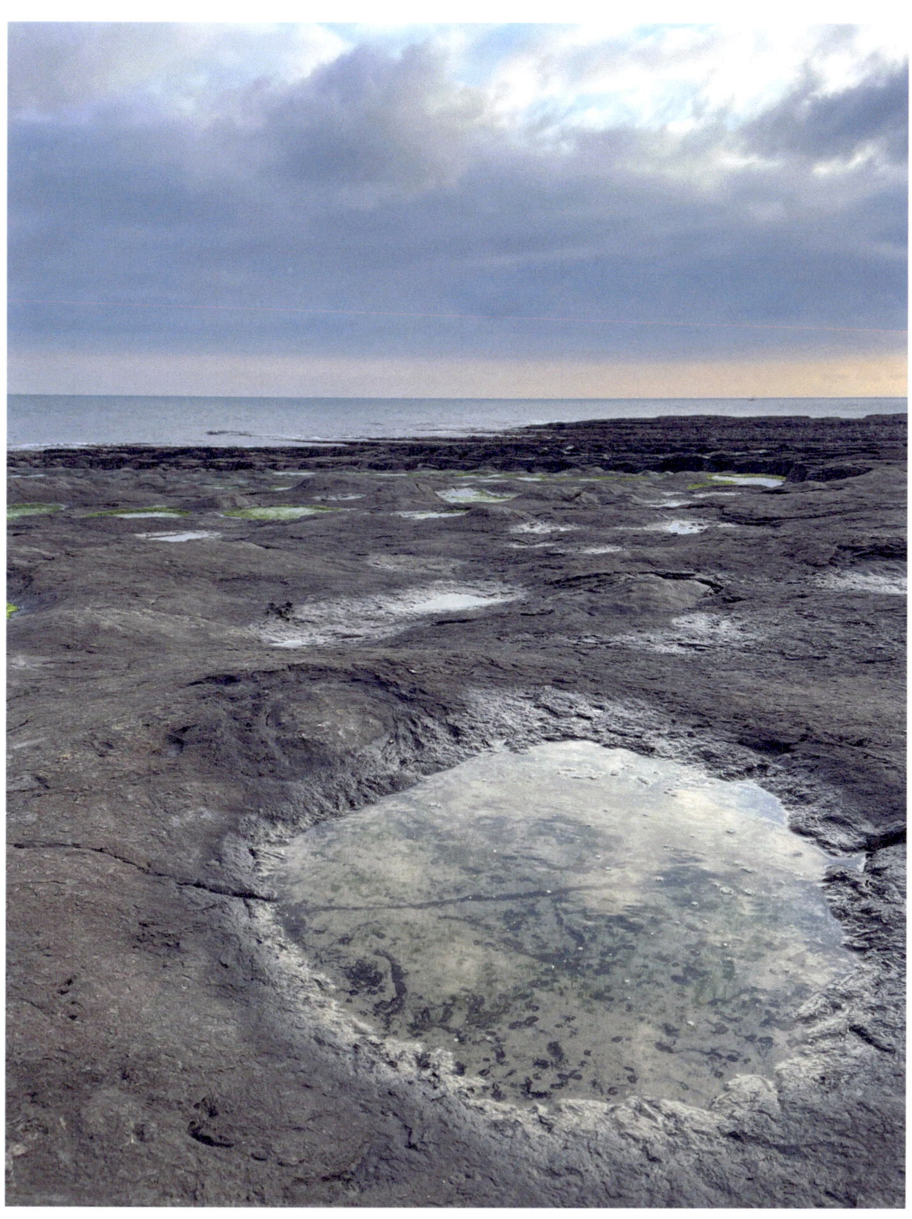

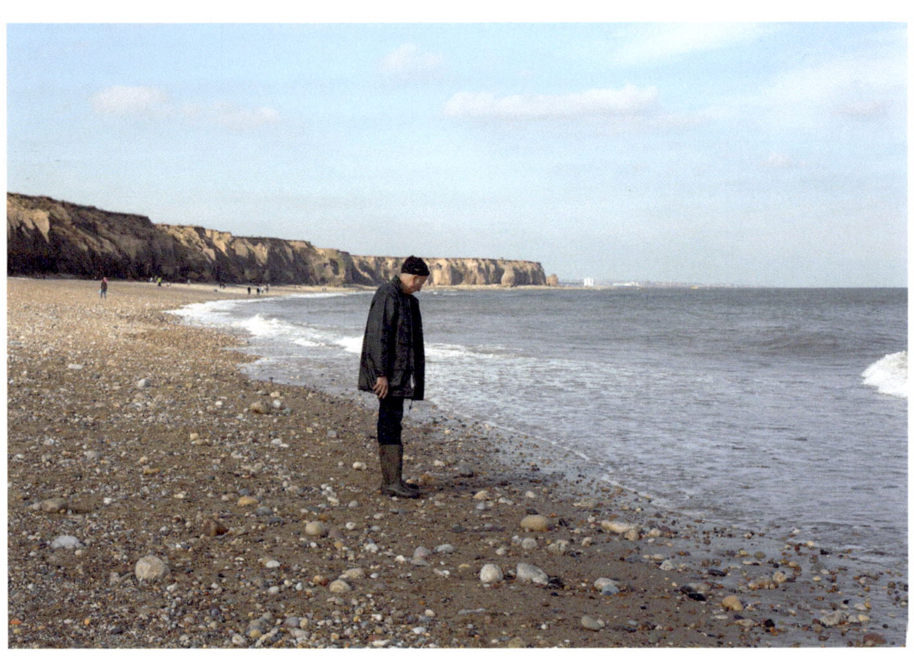

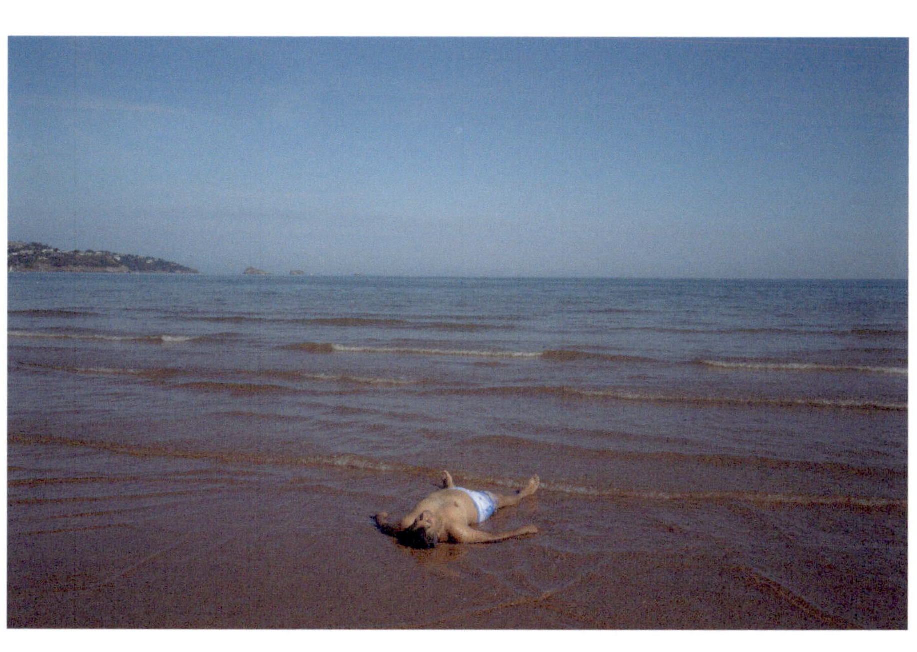

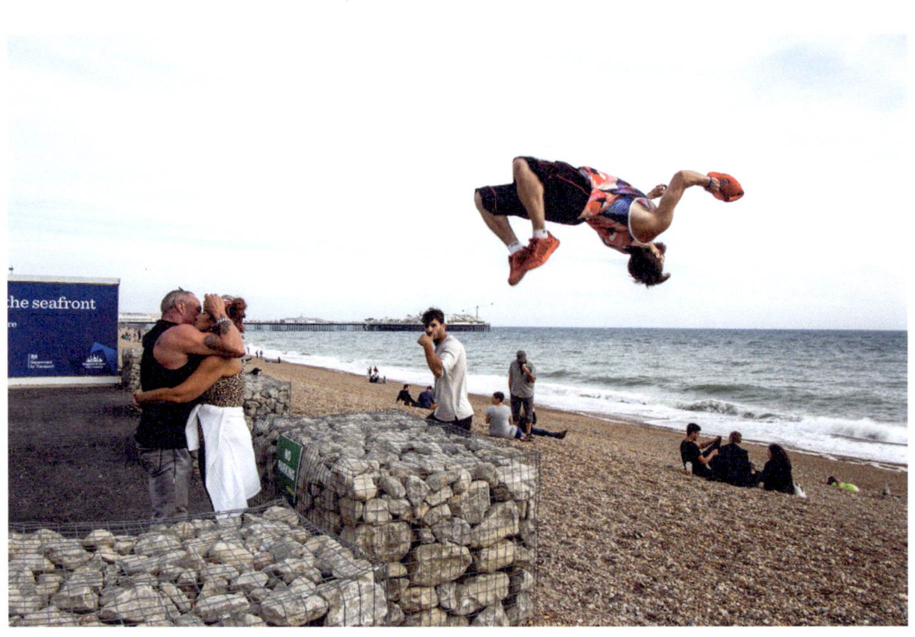
the seafront

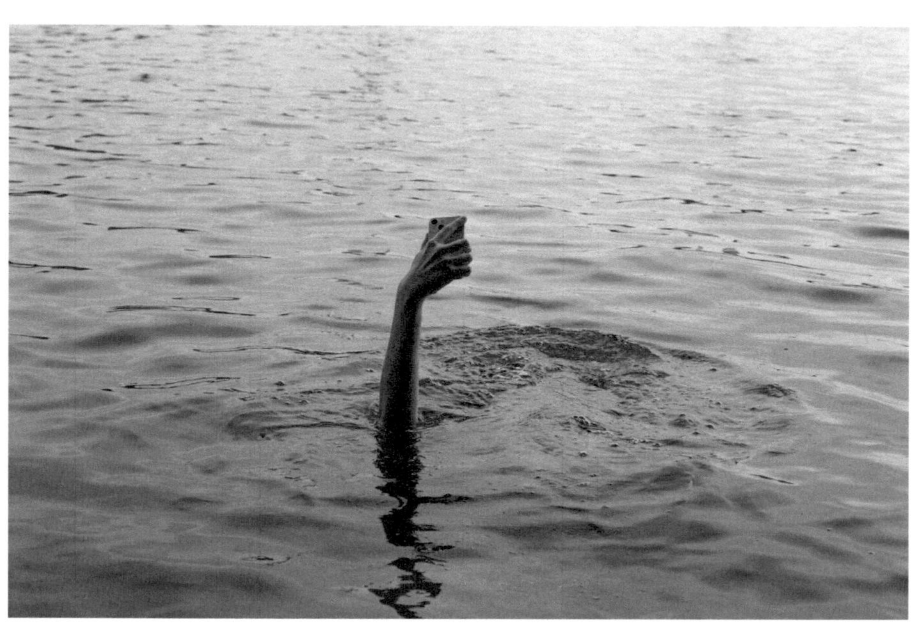

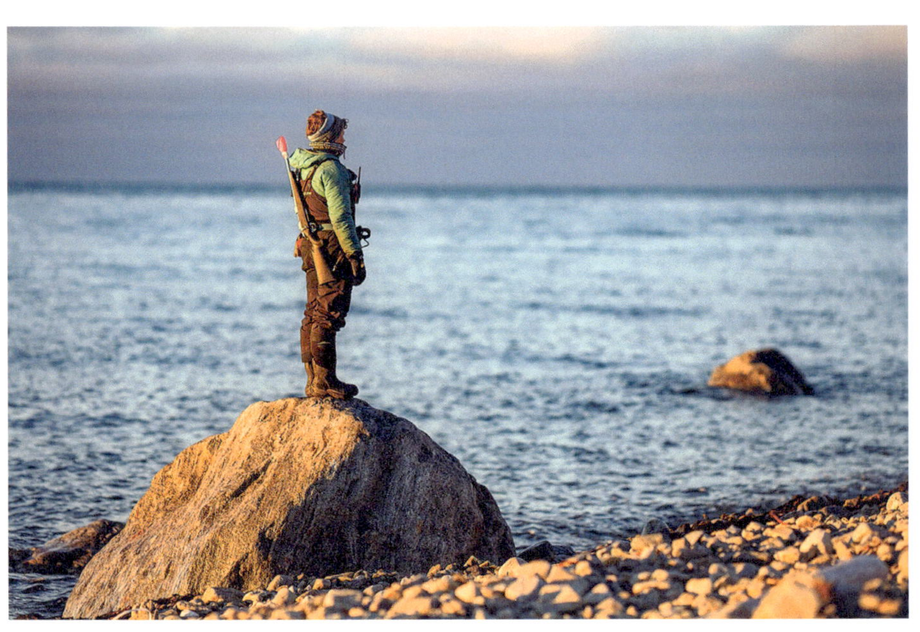

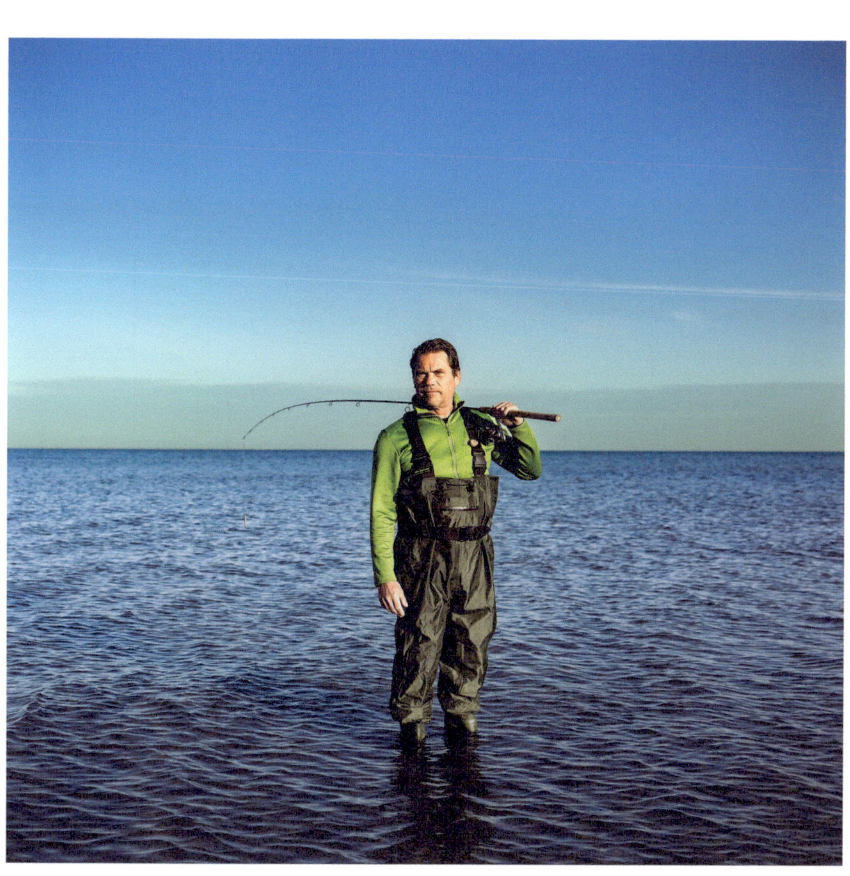

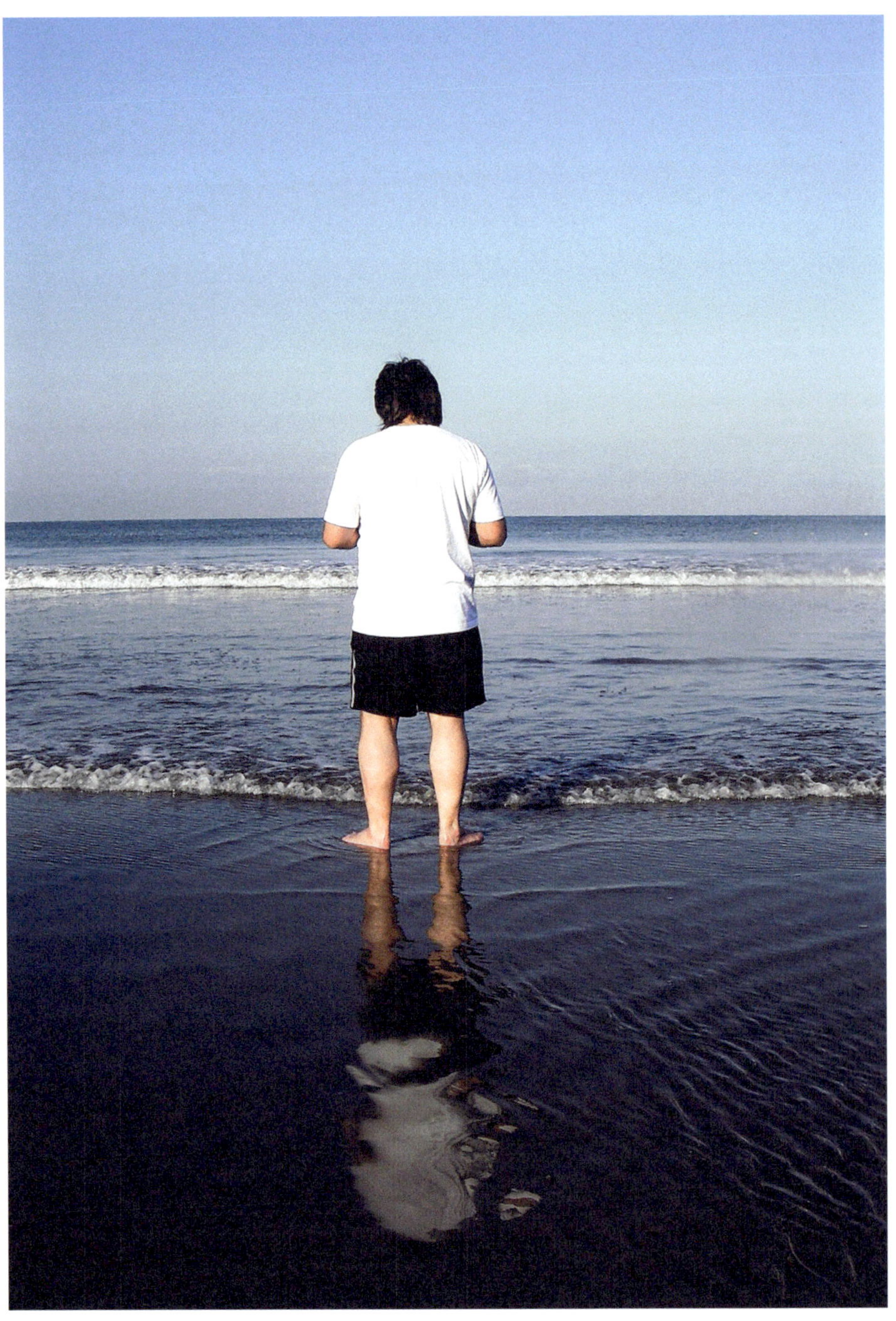

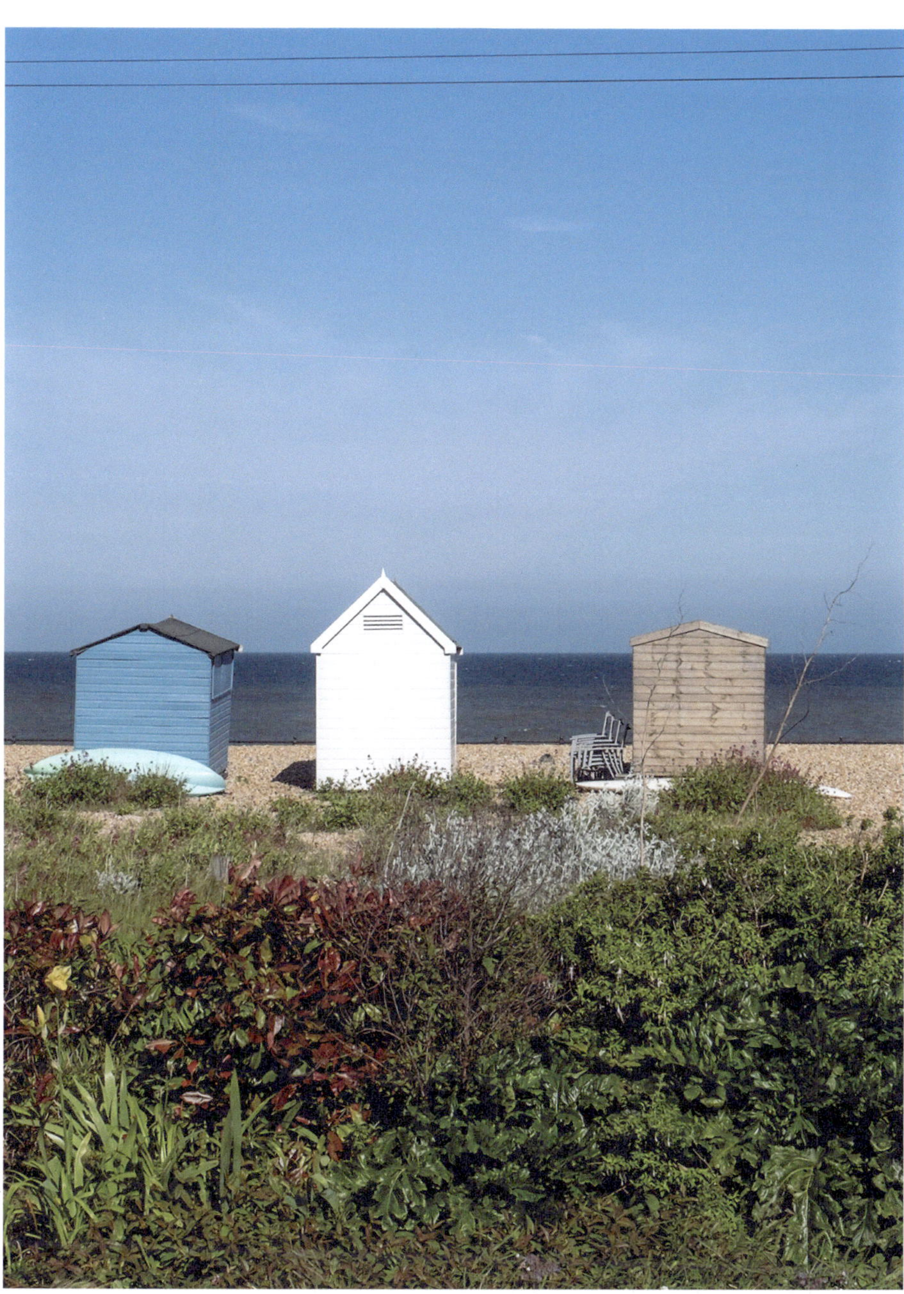

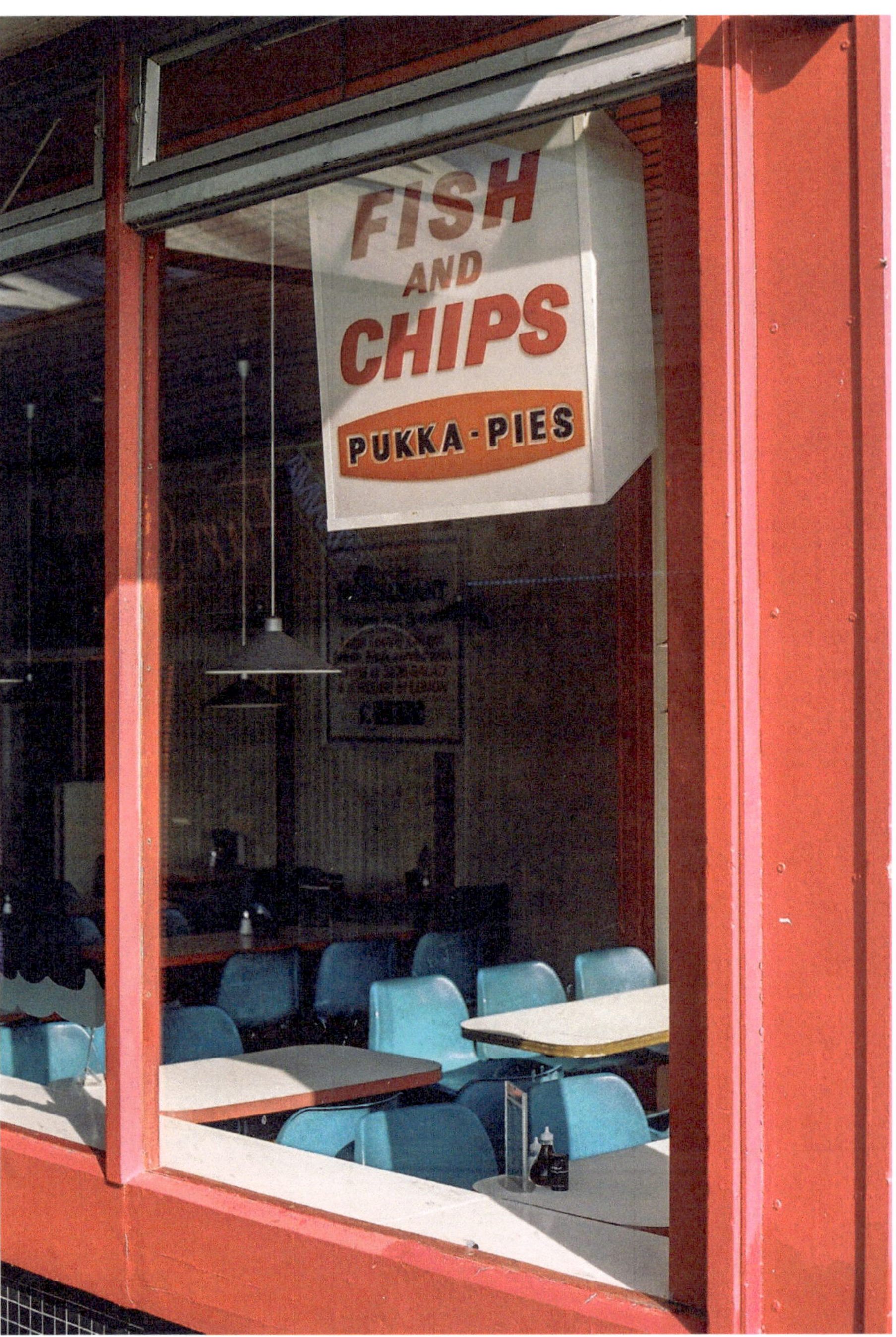
FISH
AND
CHIPS
PUKKA-PIES

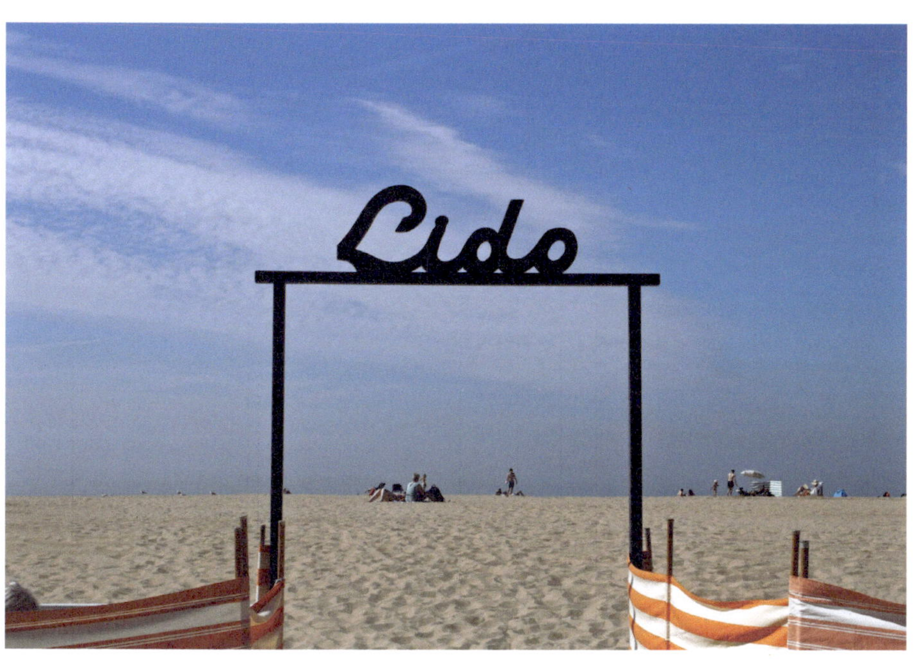
Lido

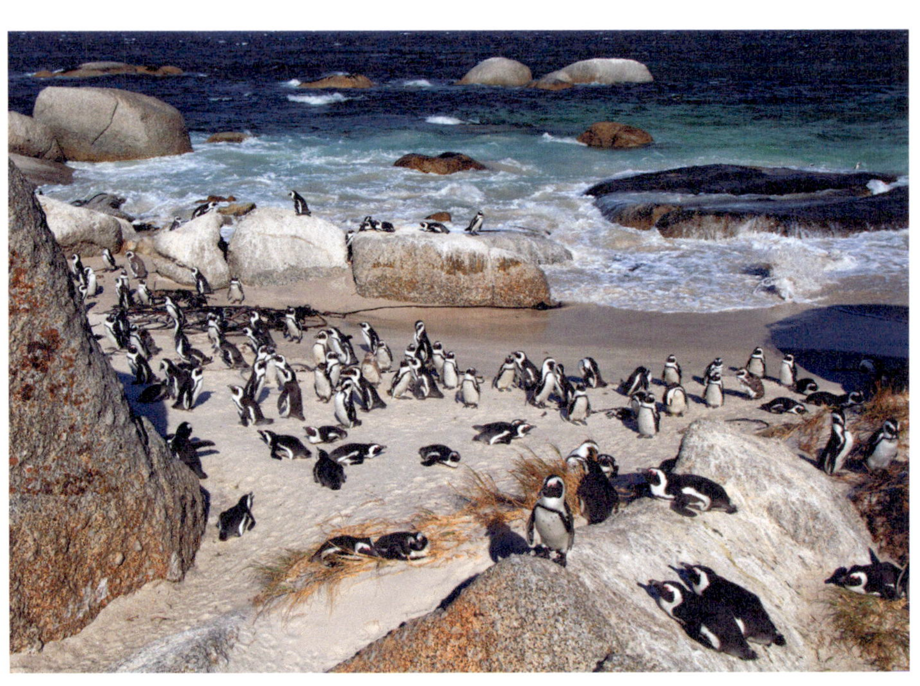

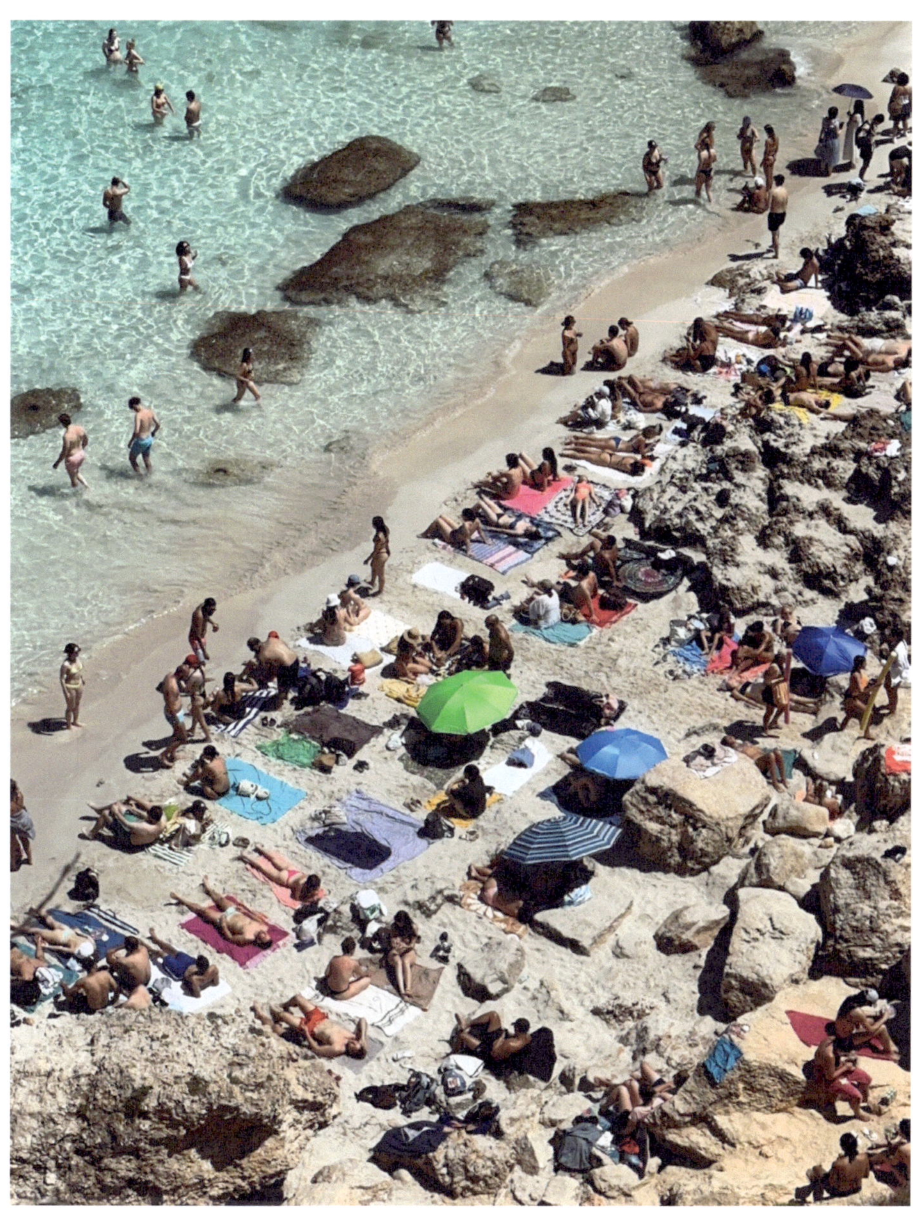

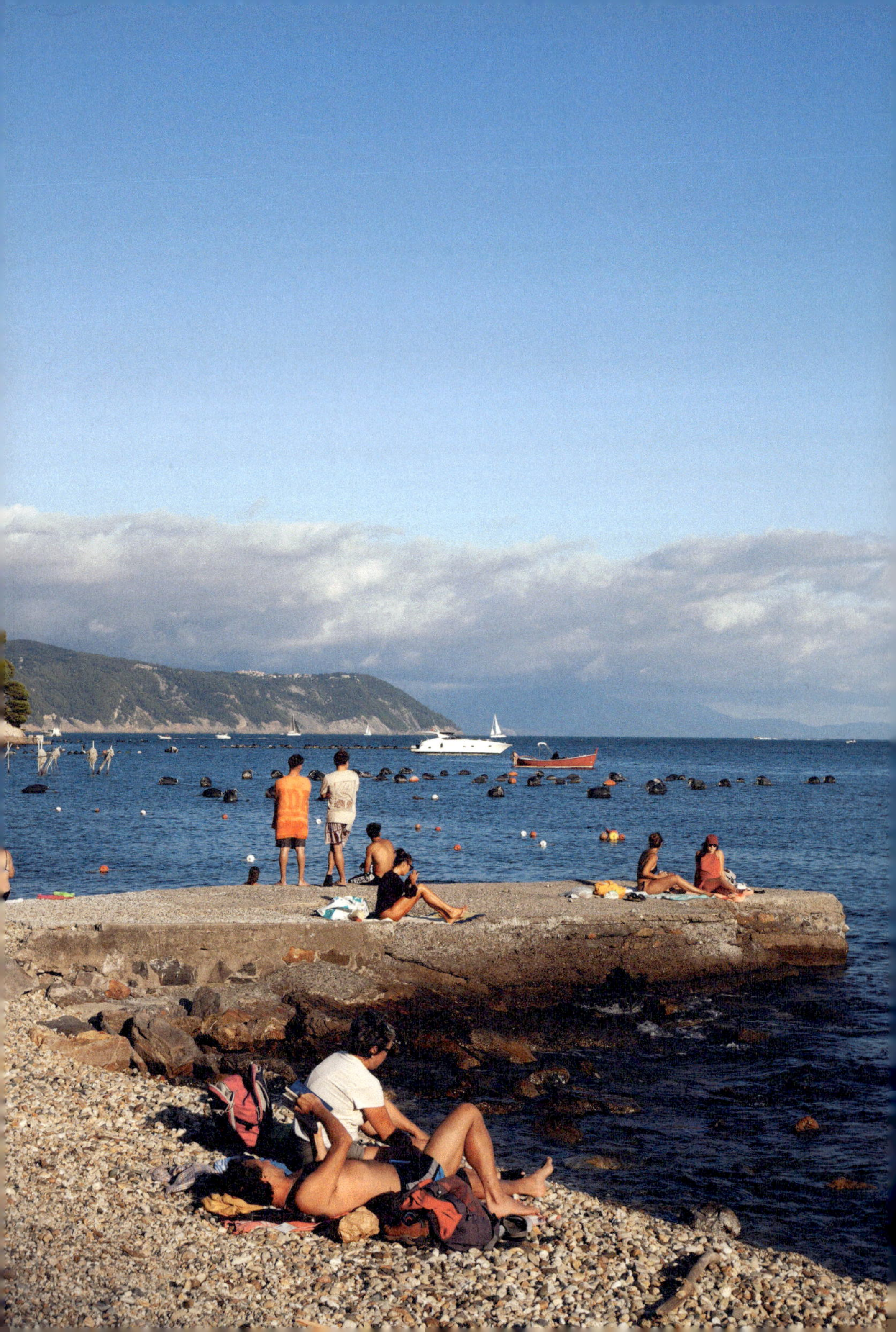

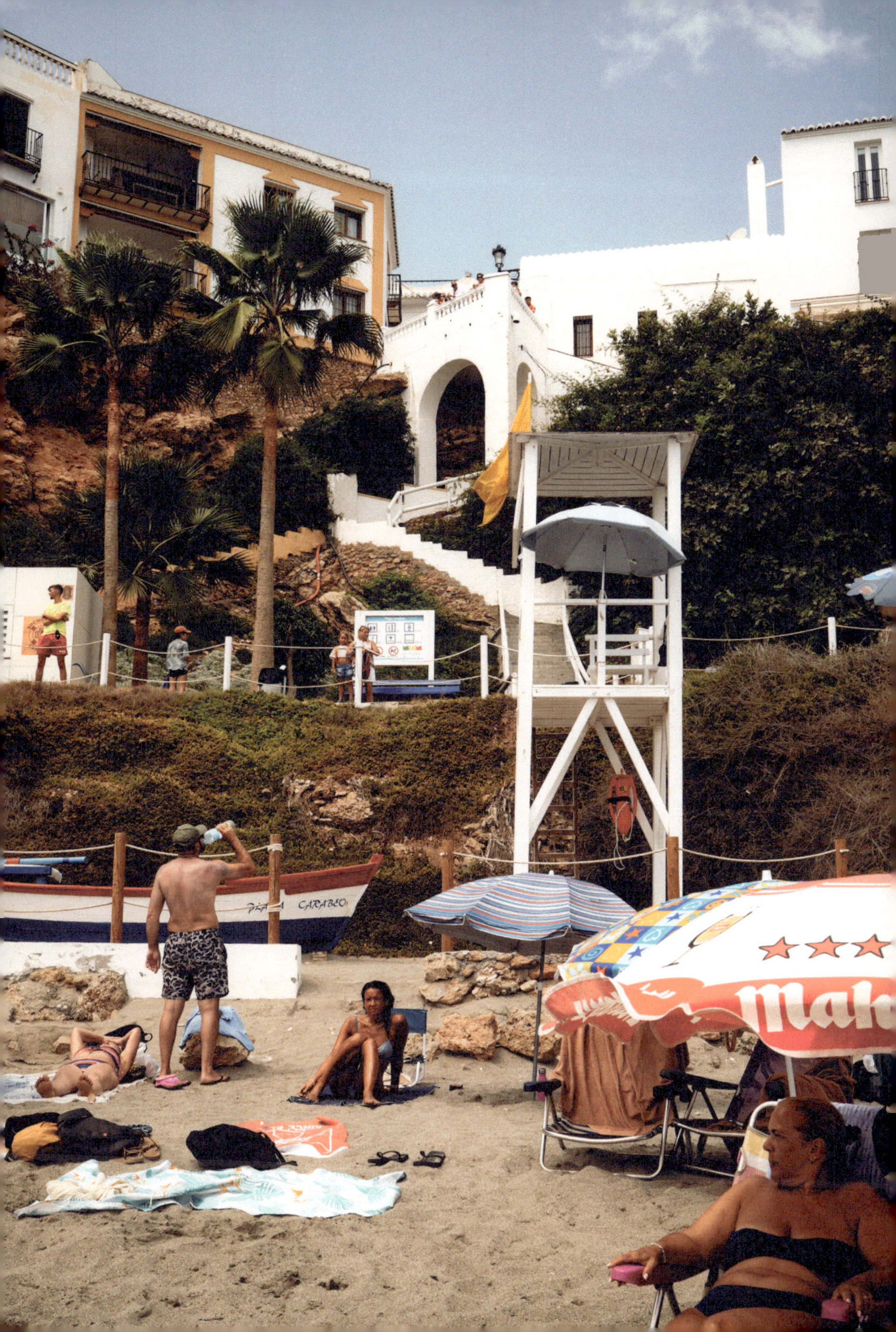
CARABEO

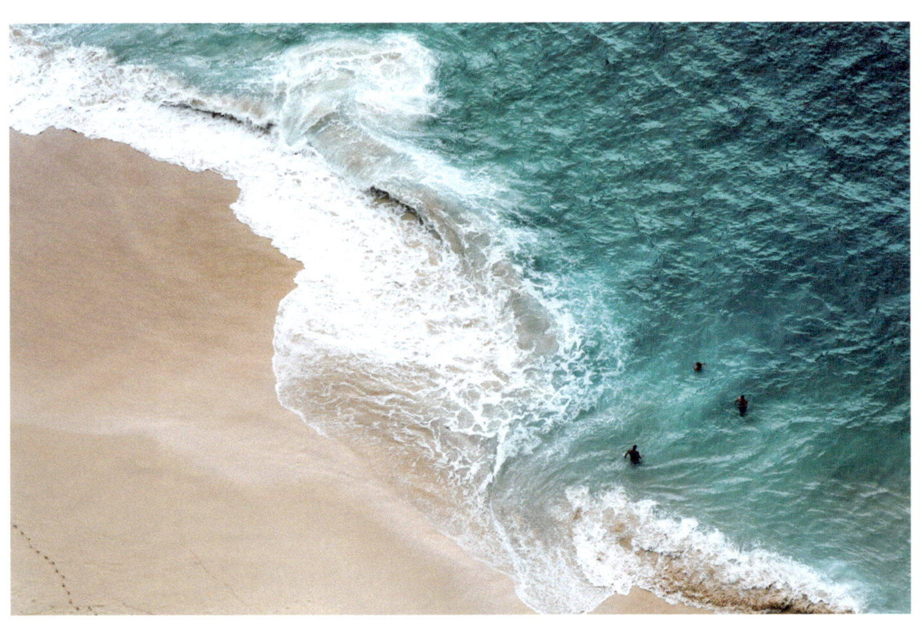

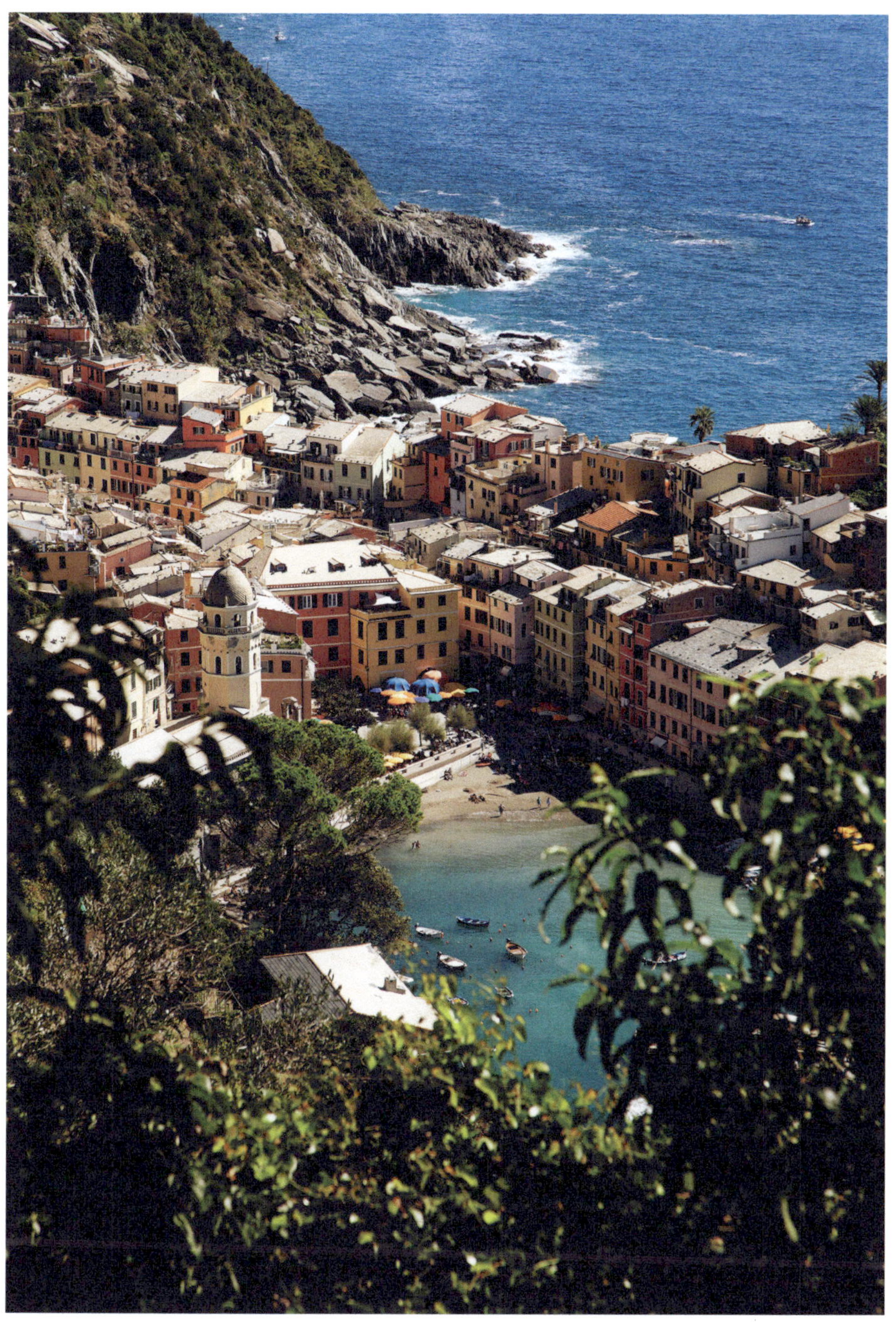

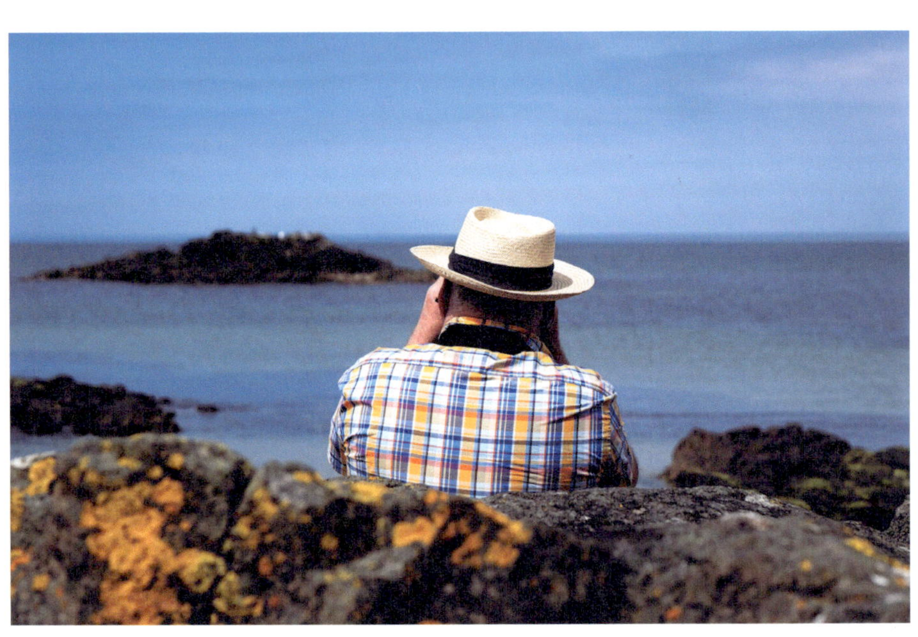

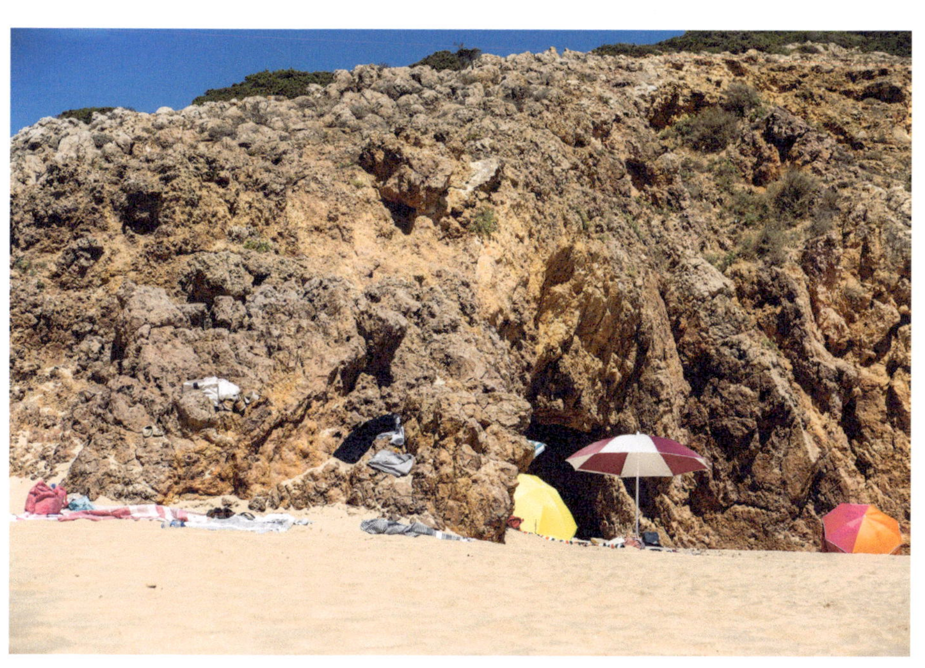

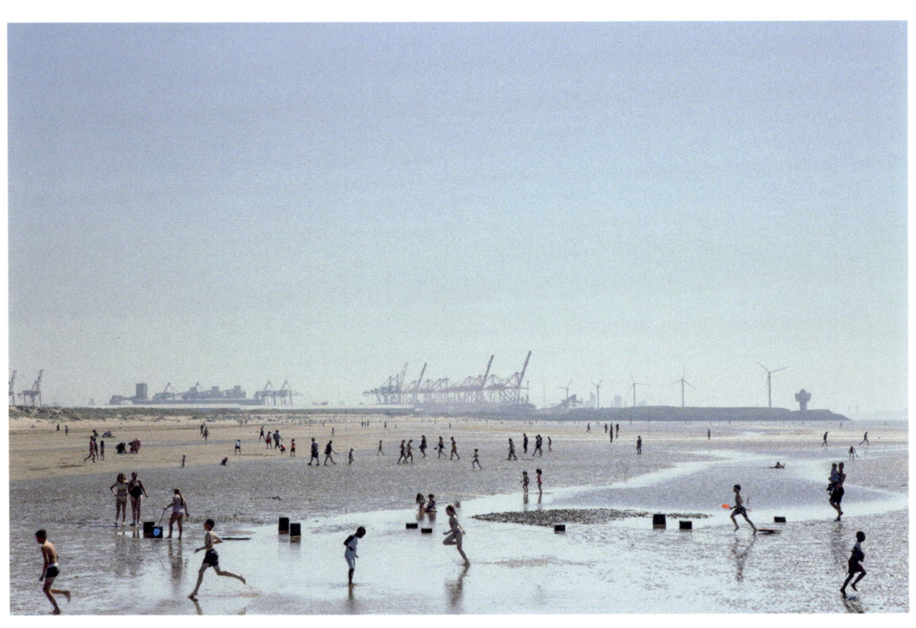

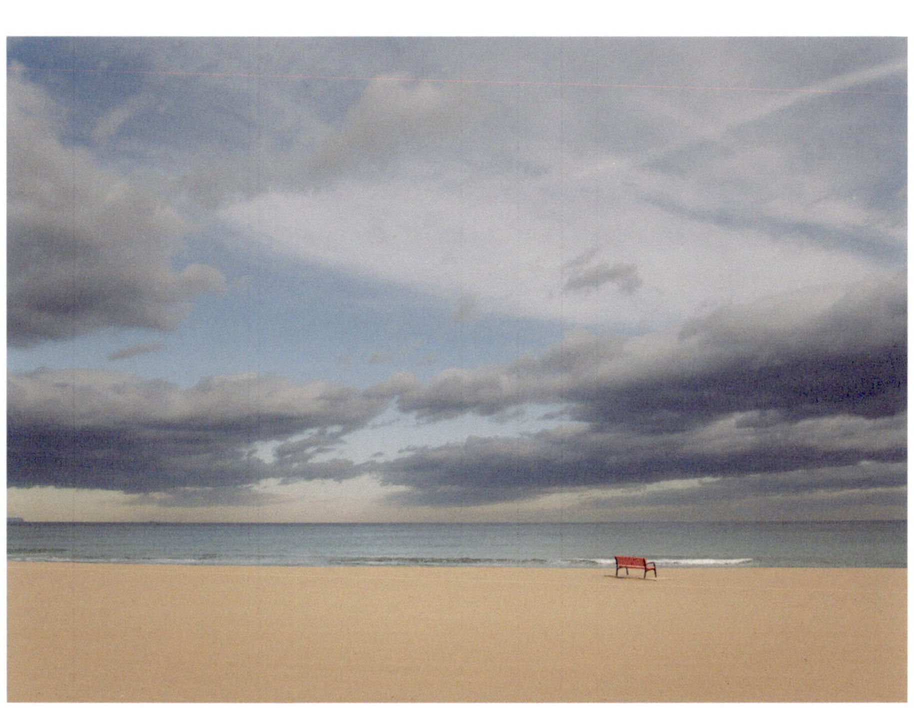

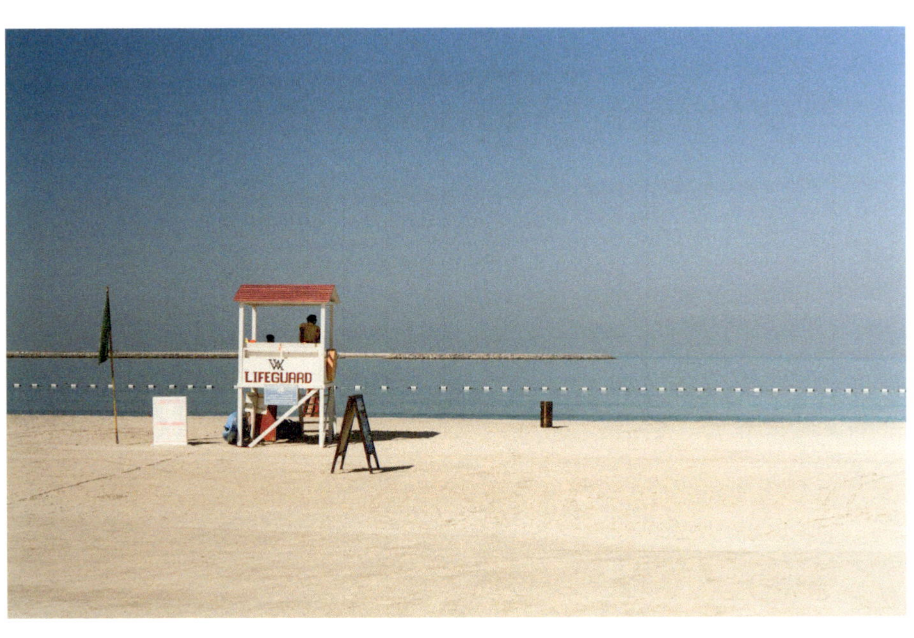
LIFEGUARD

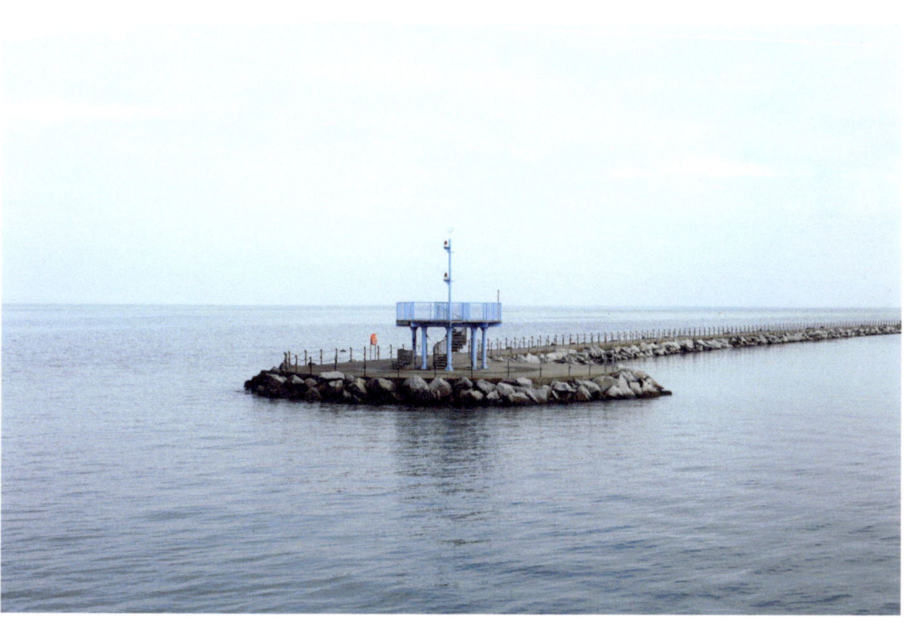

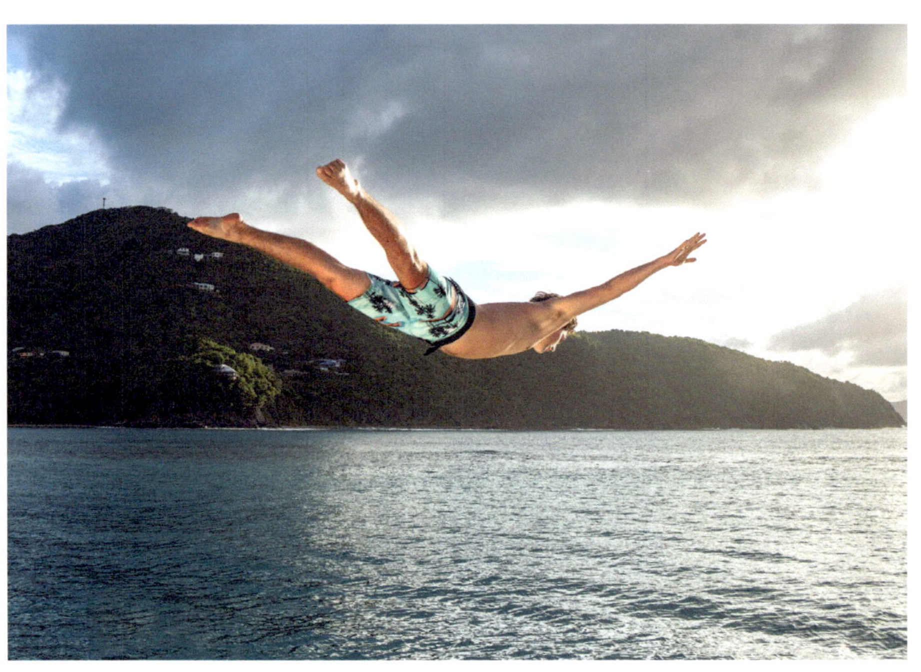

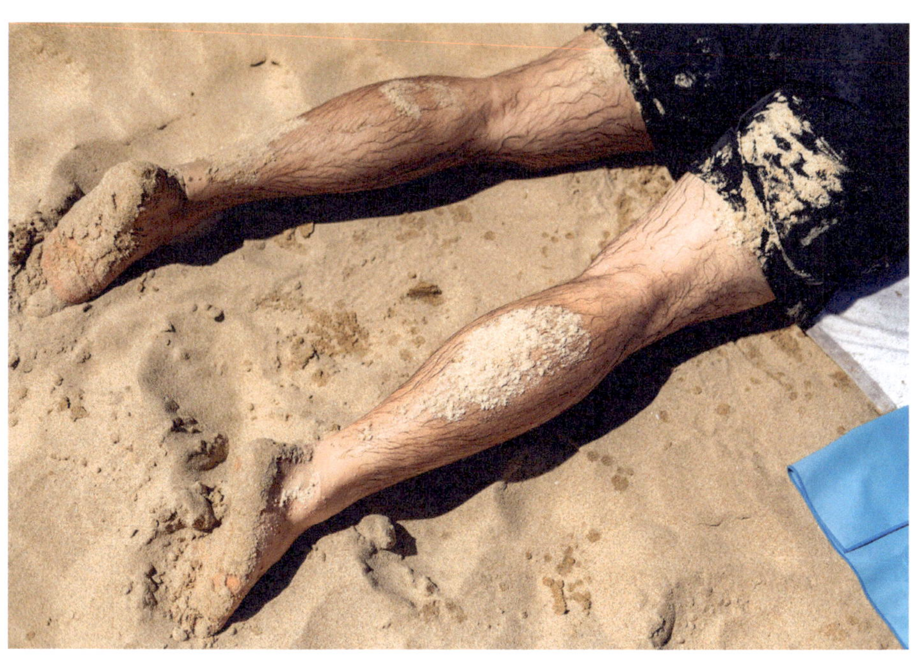

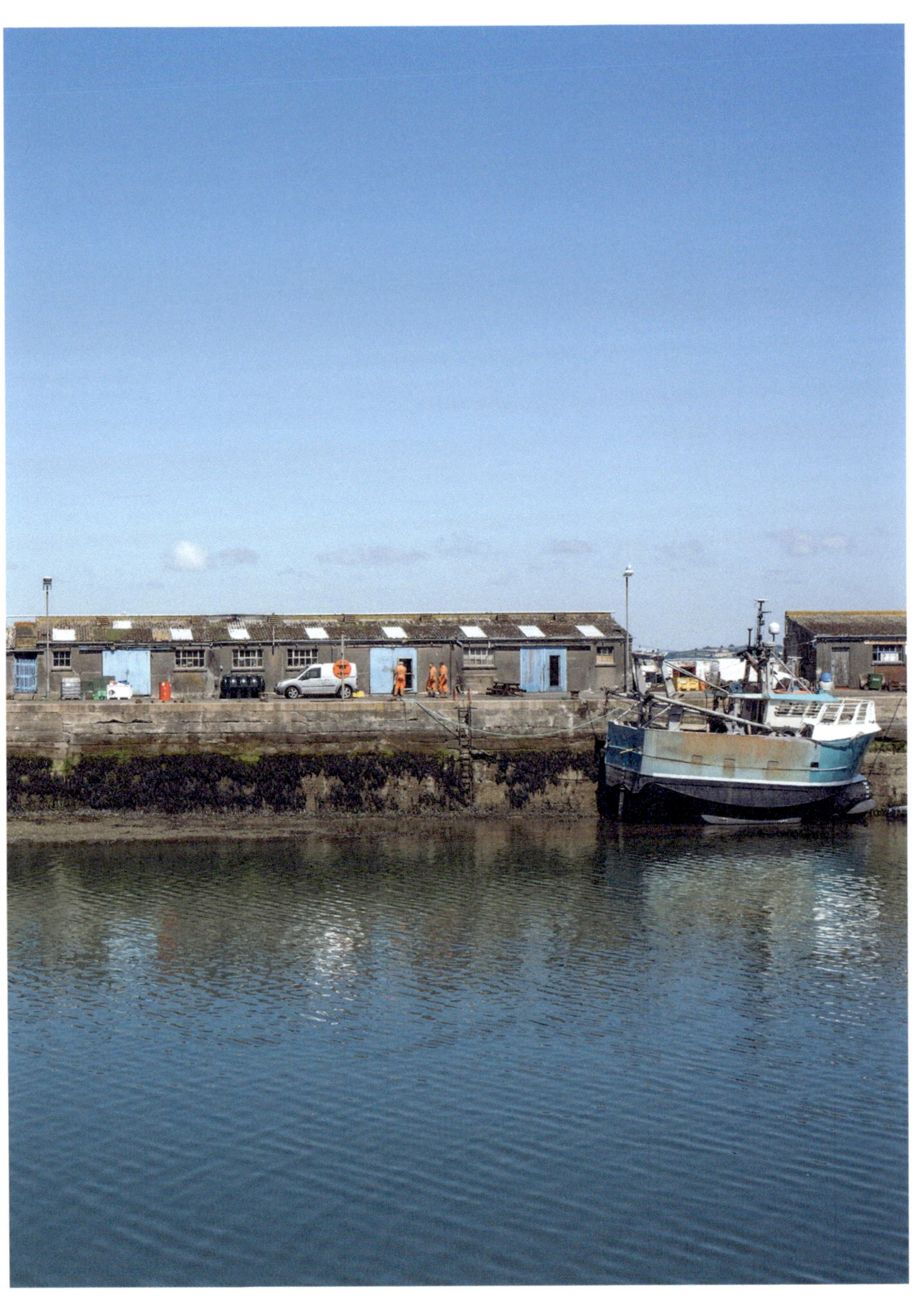

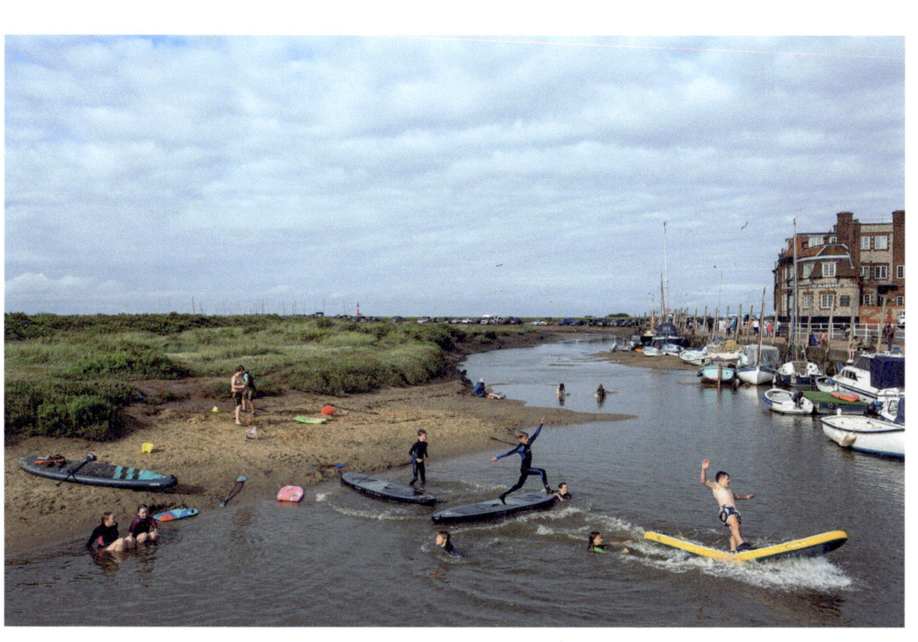

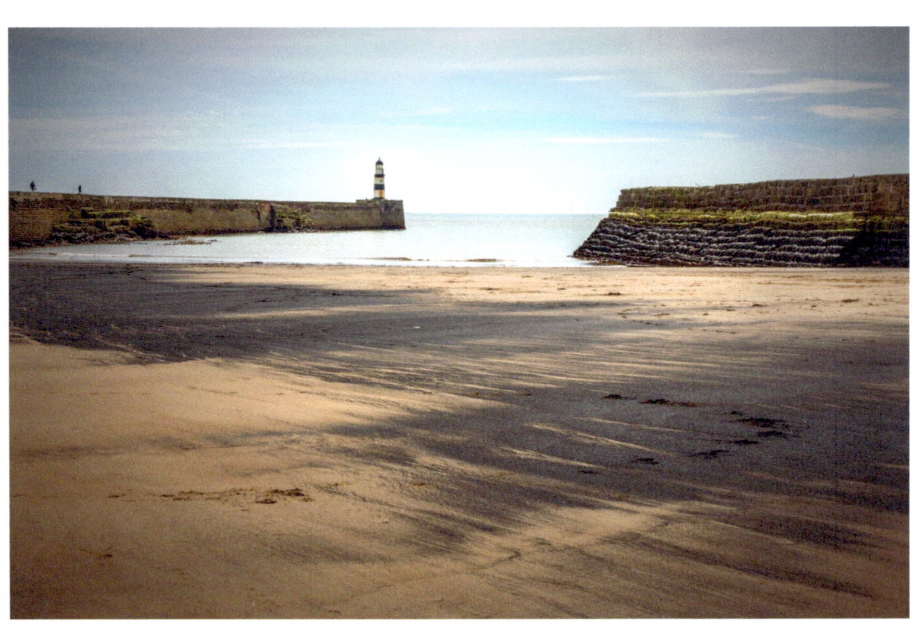

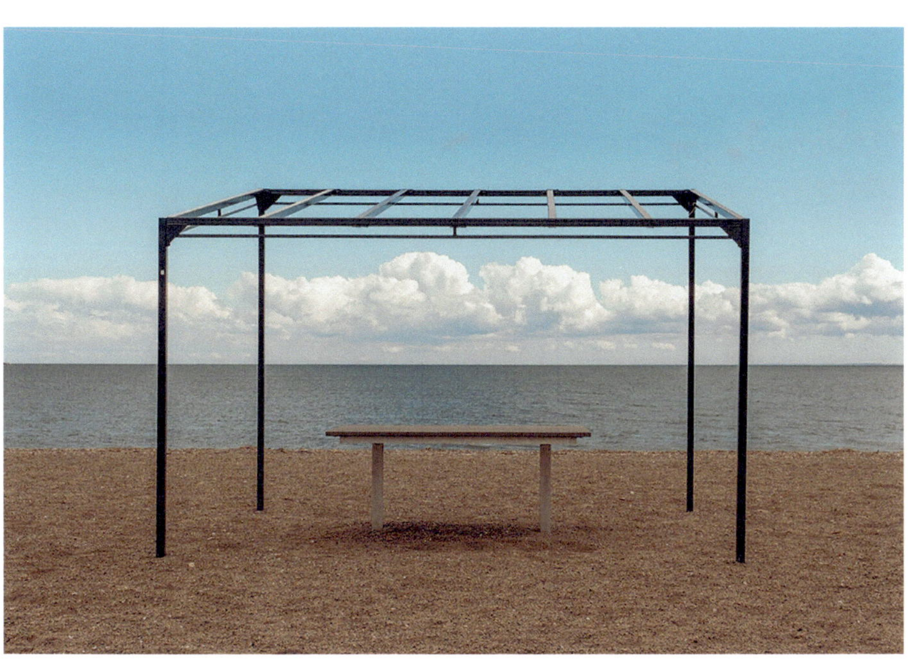

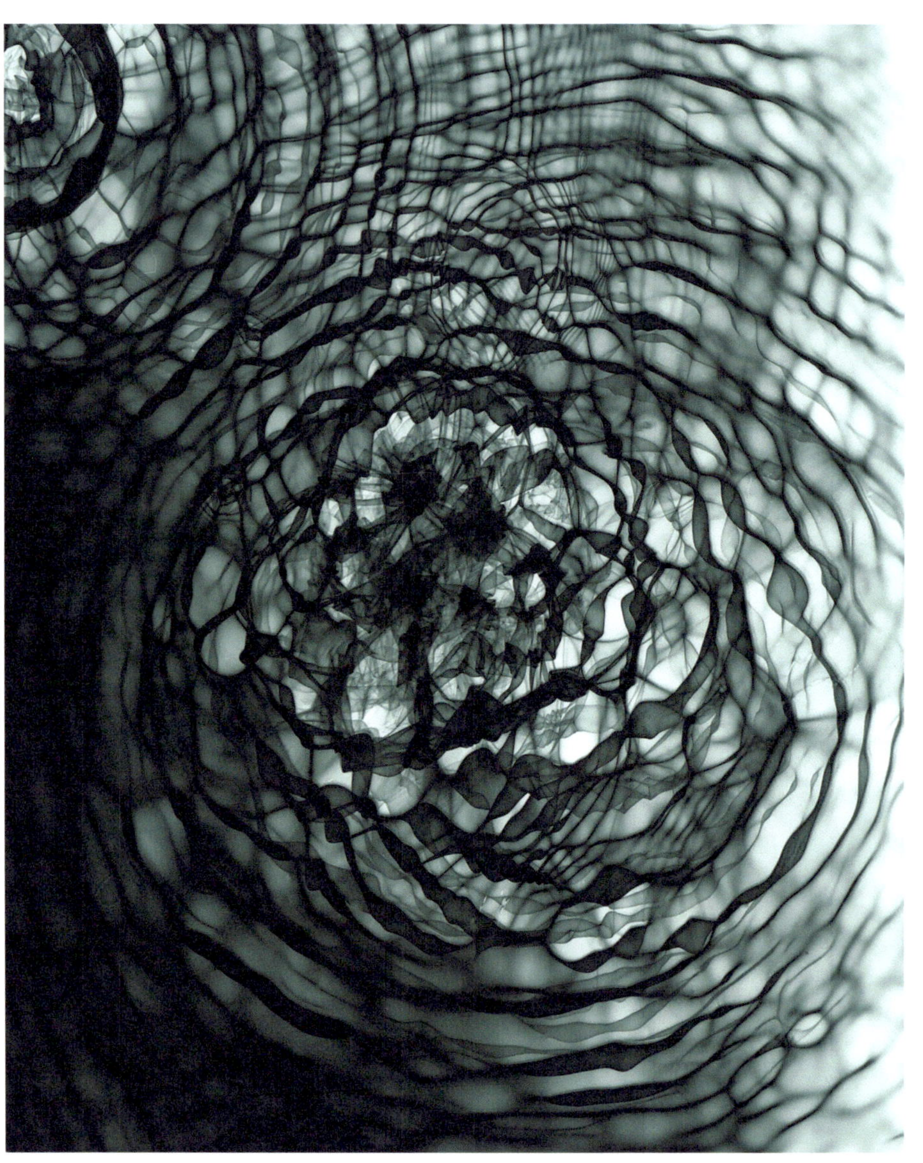

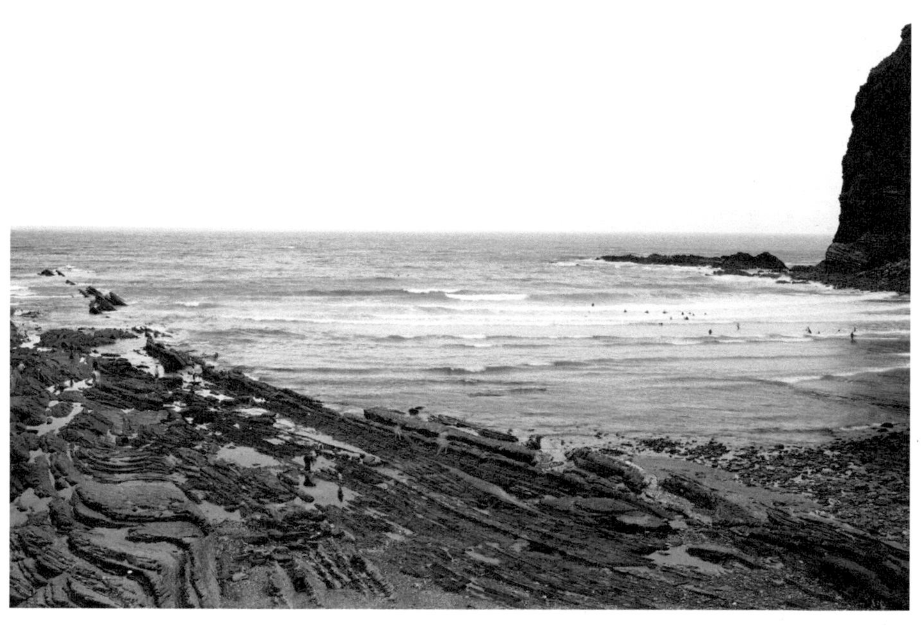

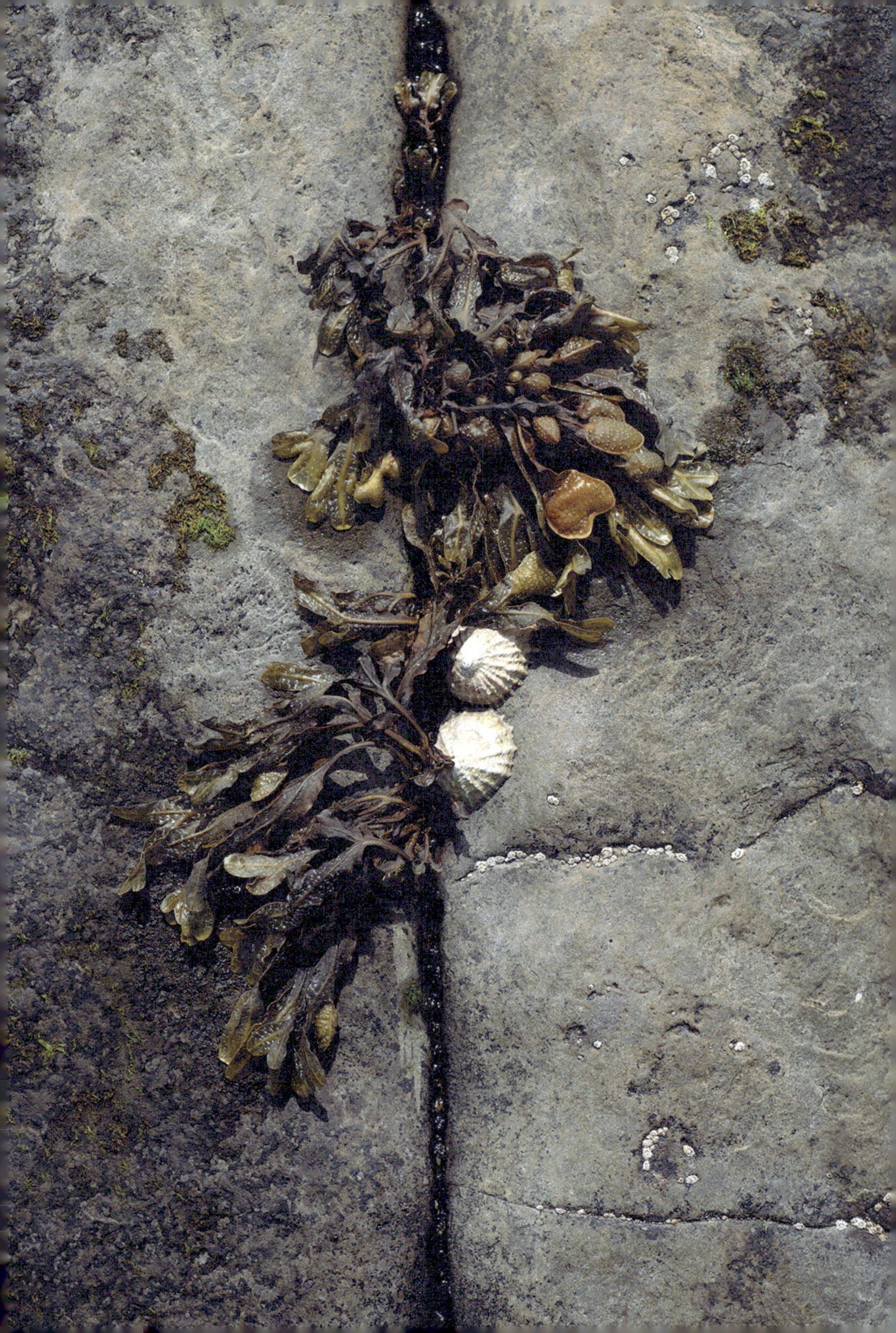

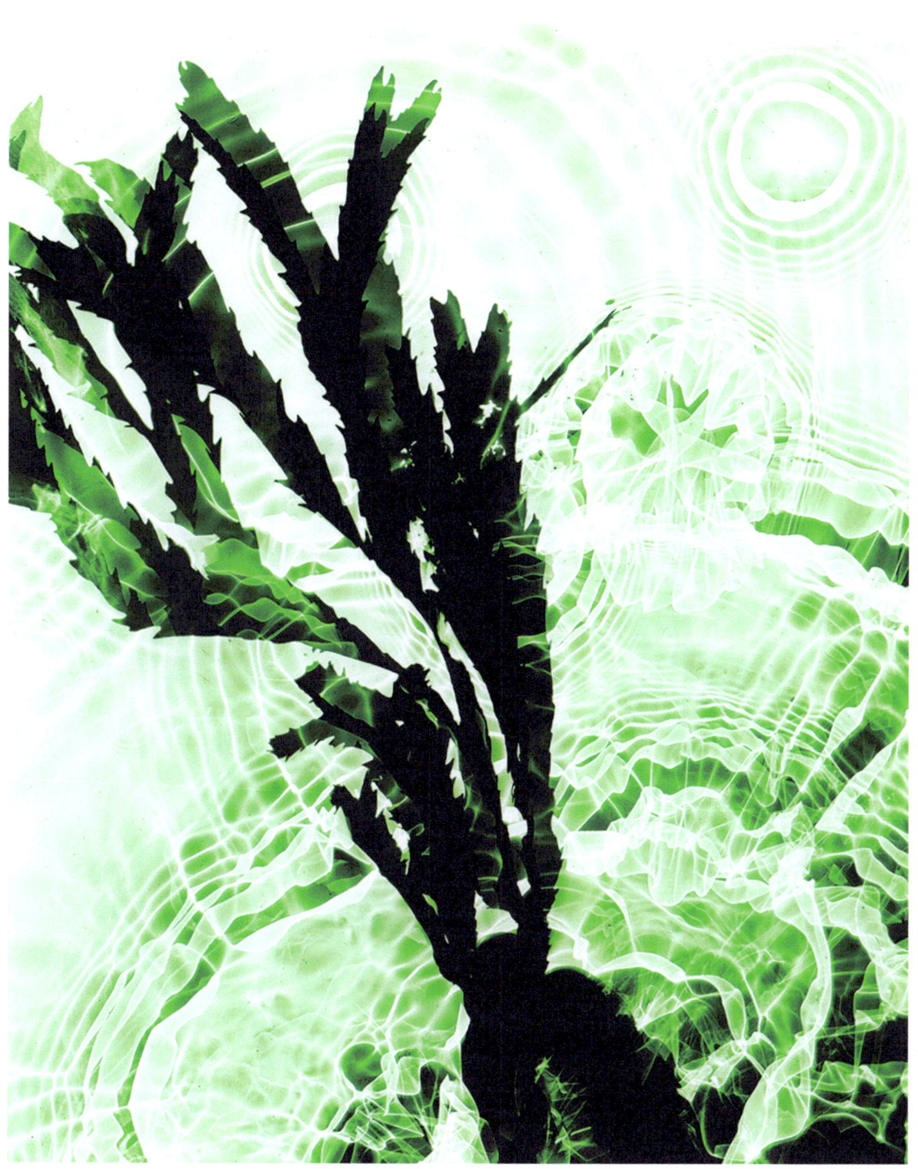

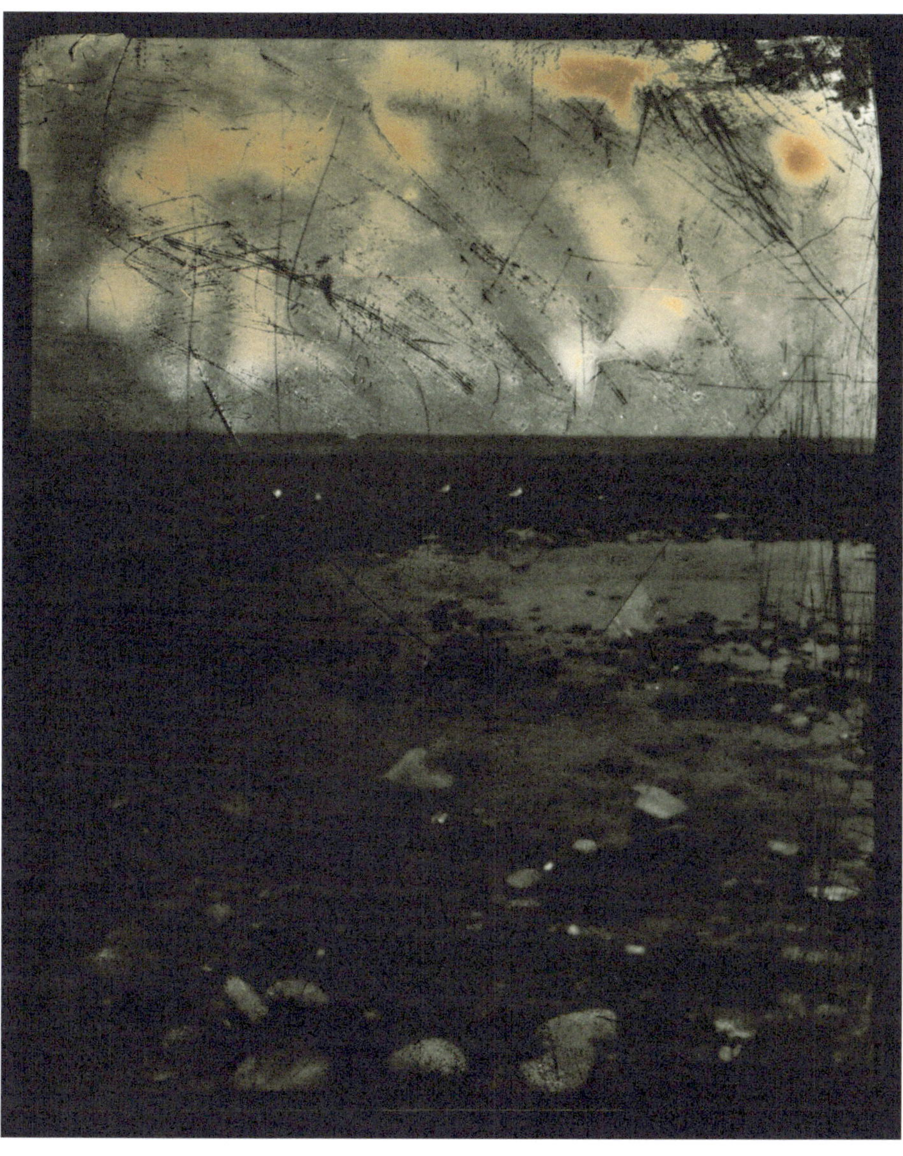

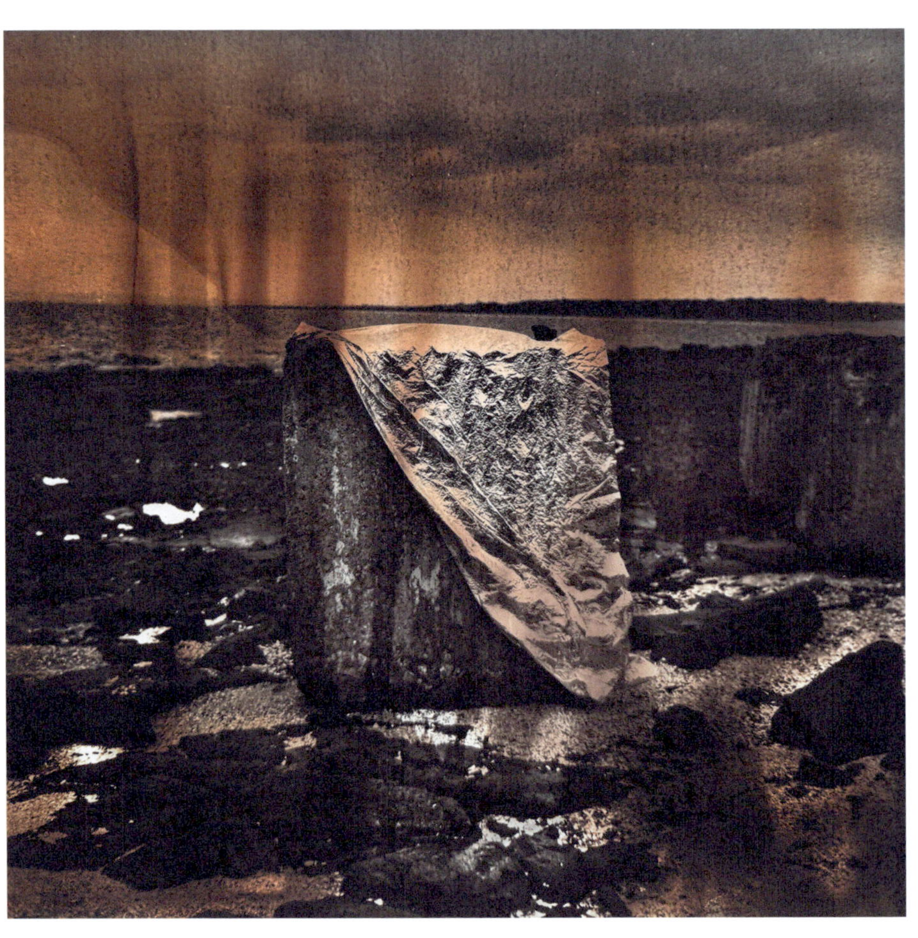

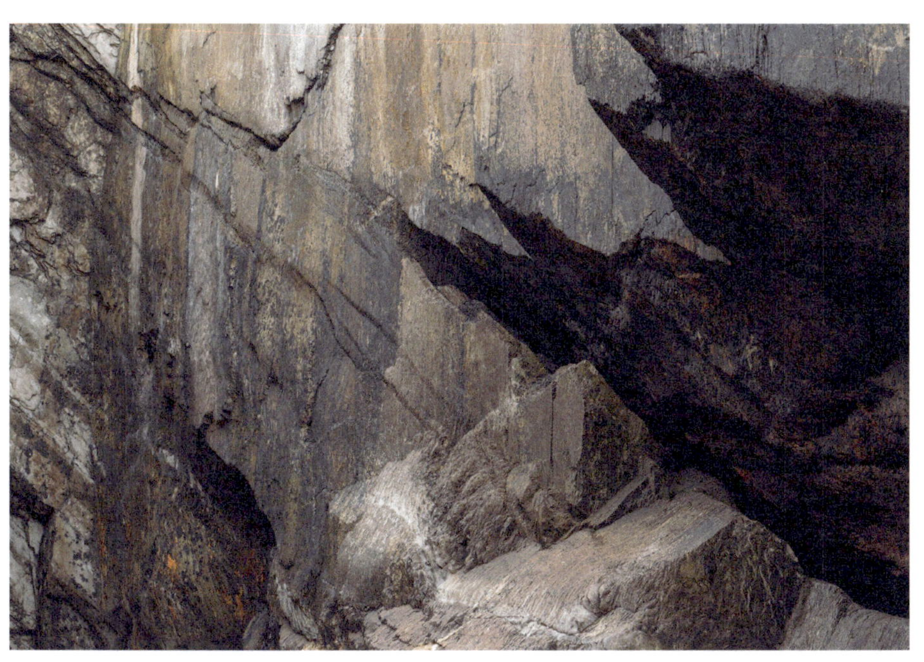

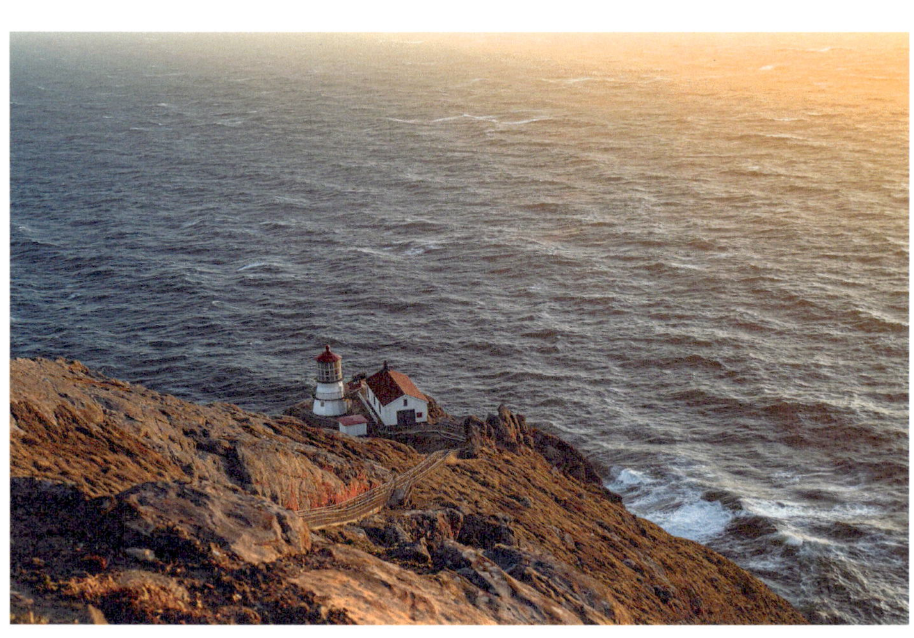

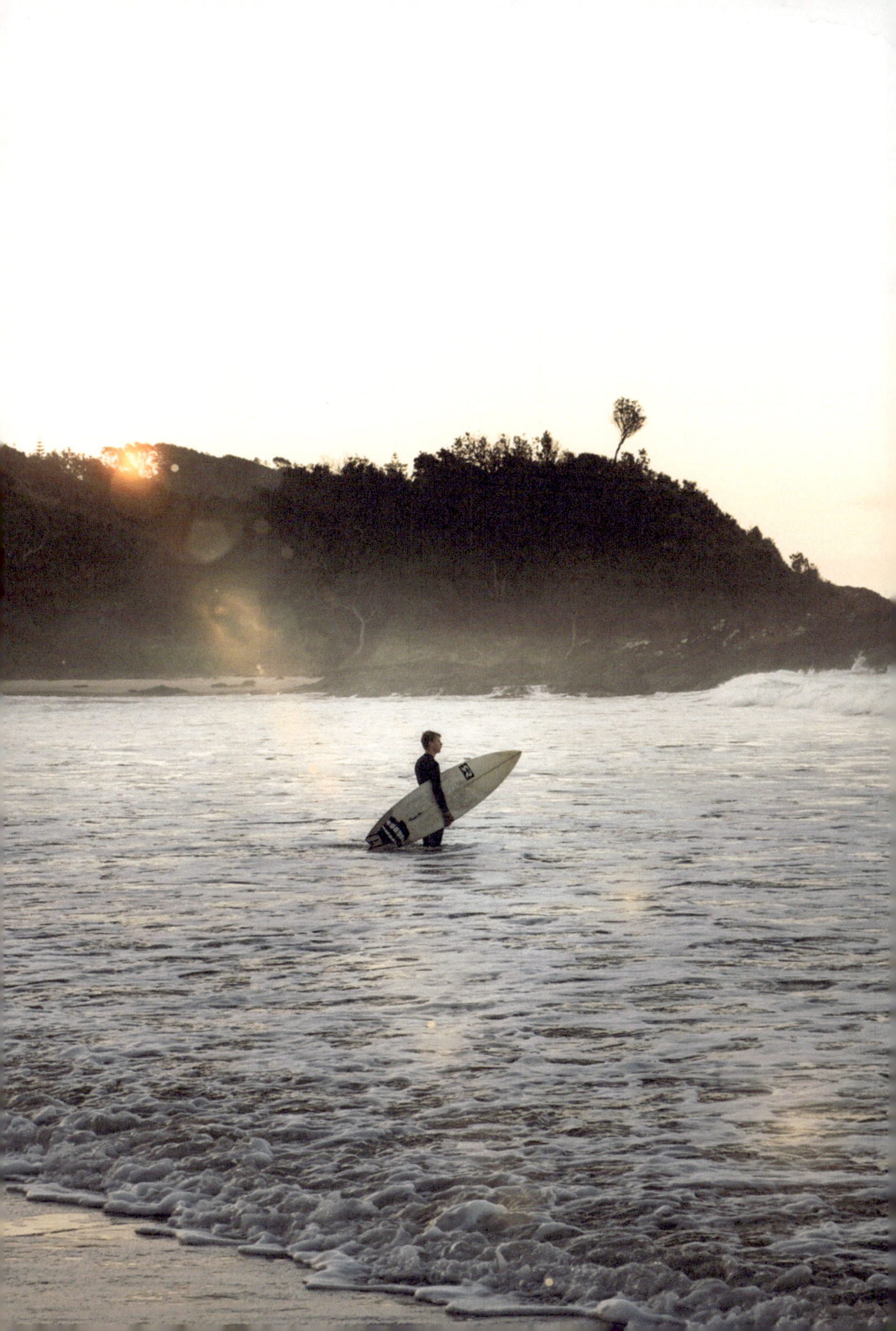

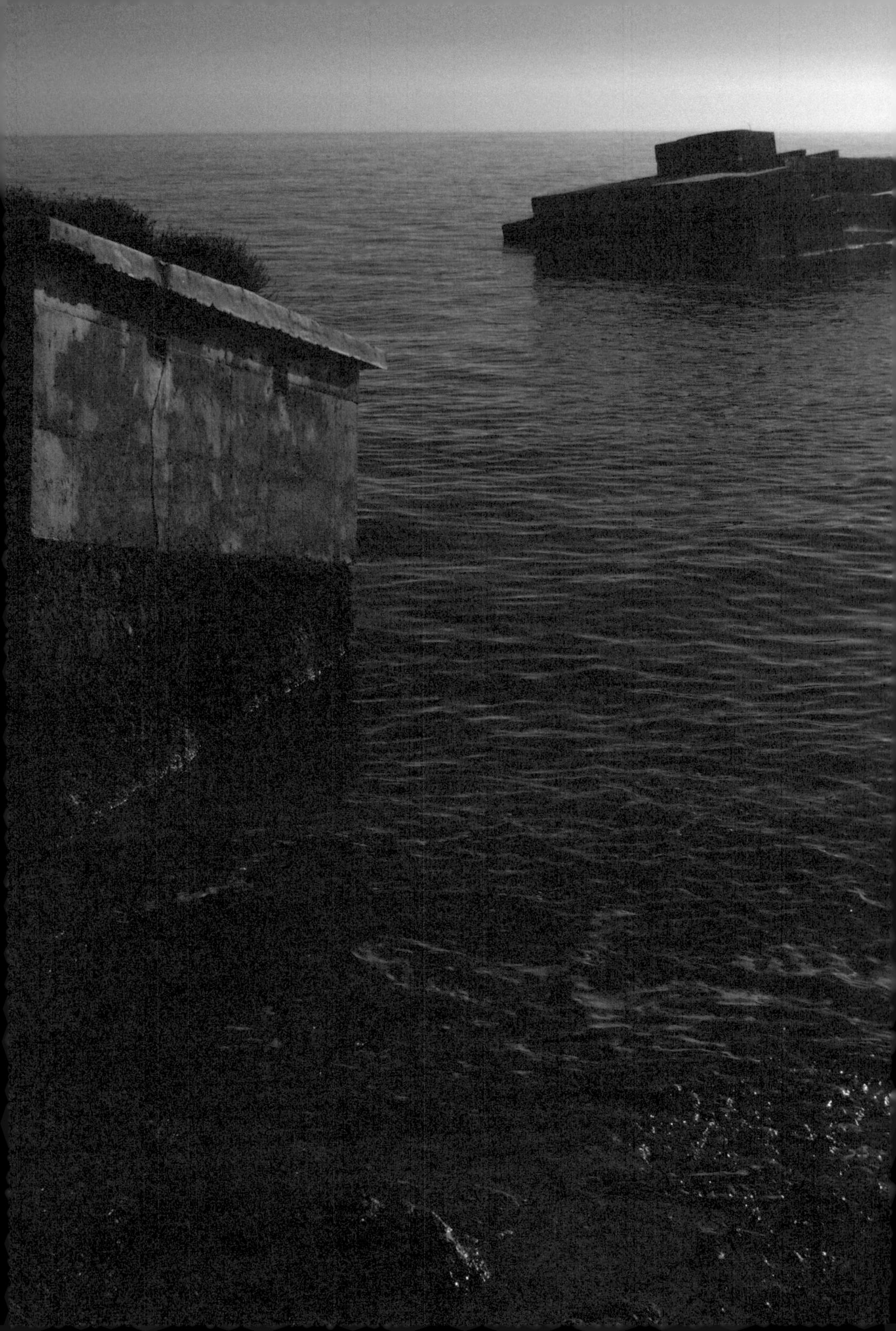

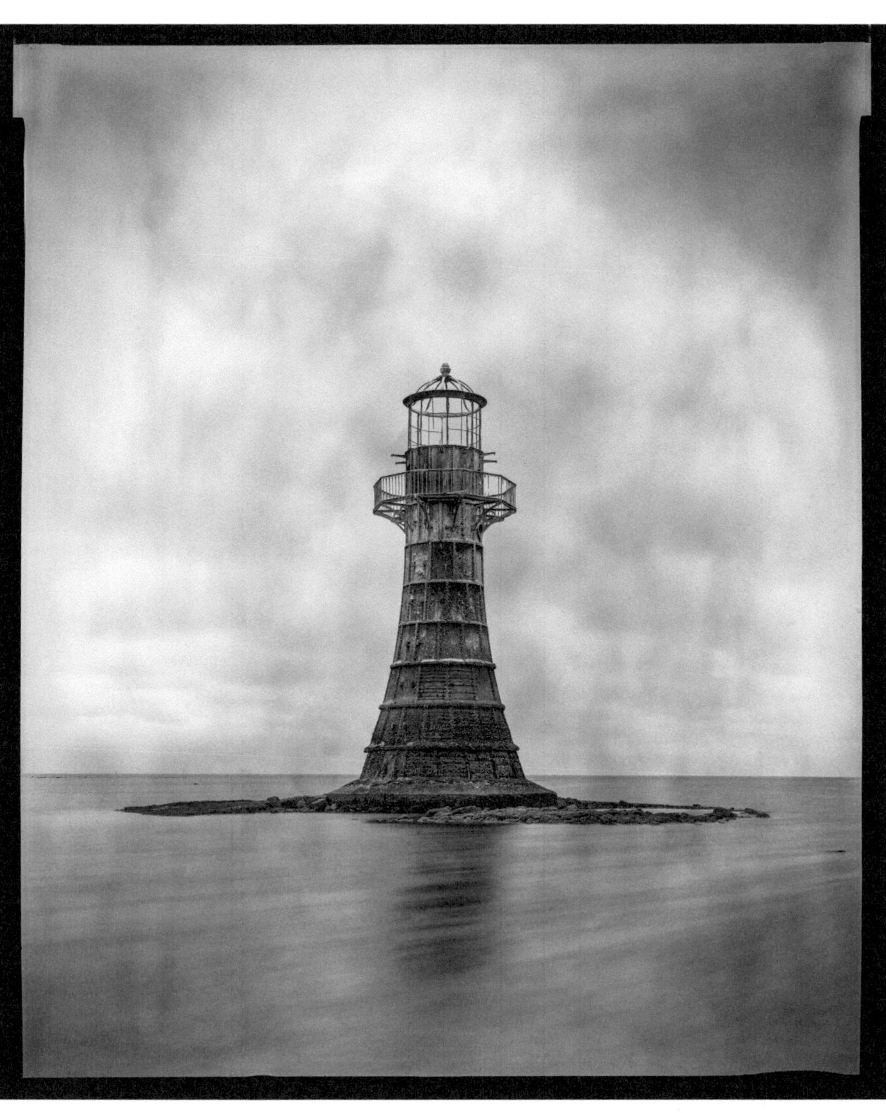

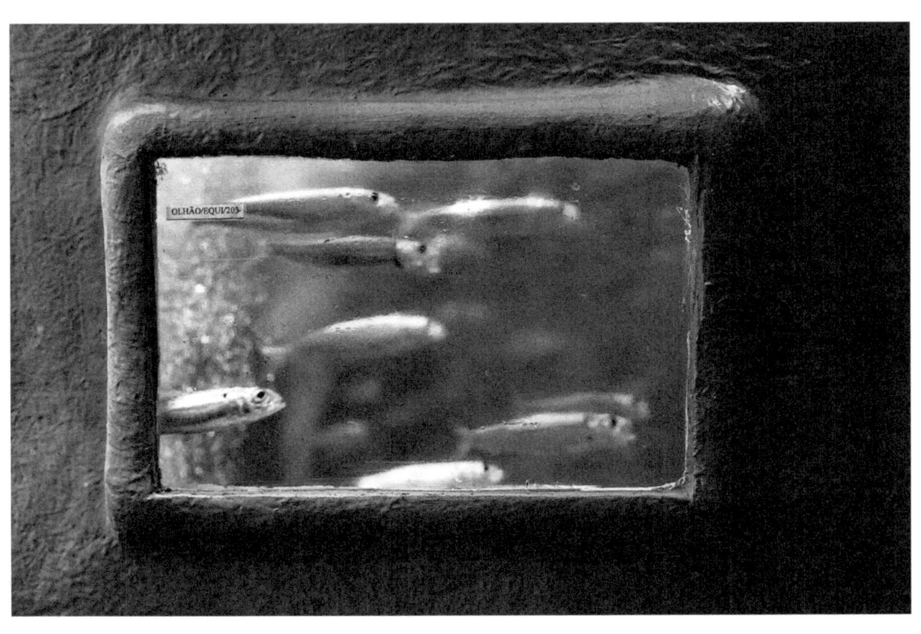
OLHÃO/EQUI/203

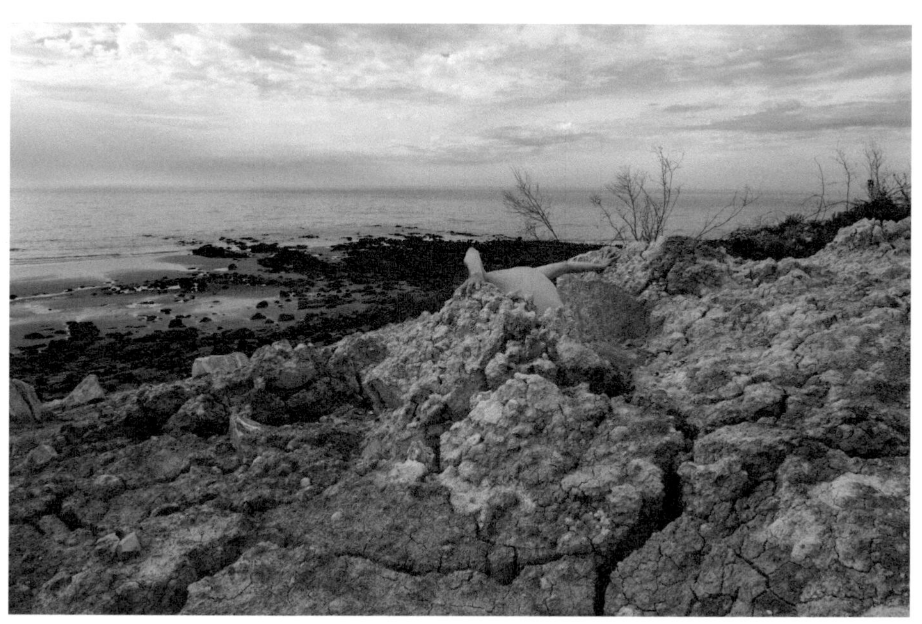

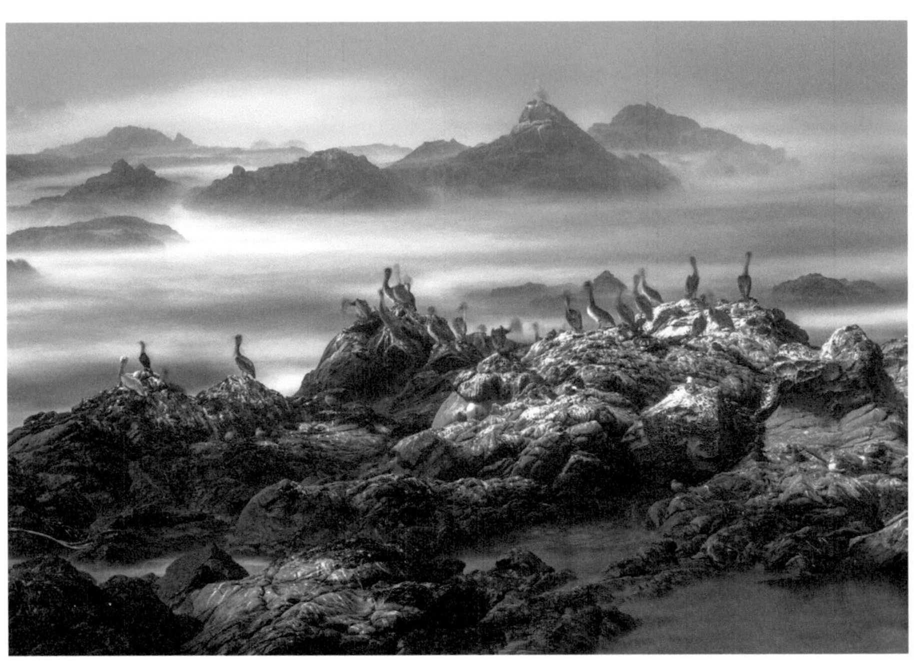

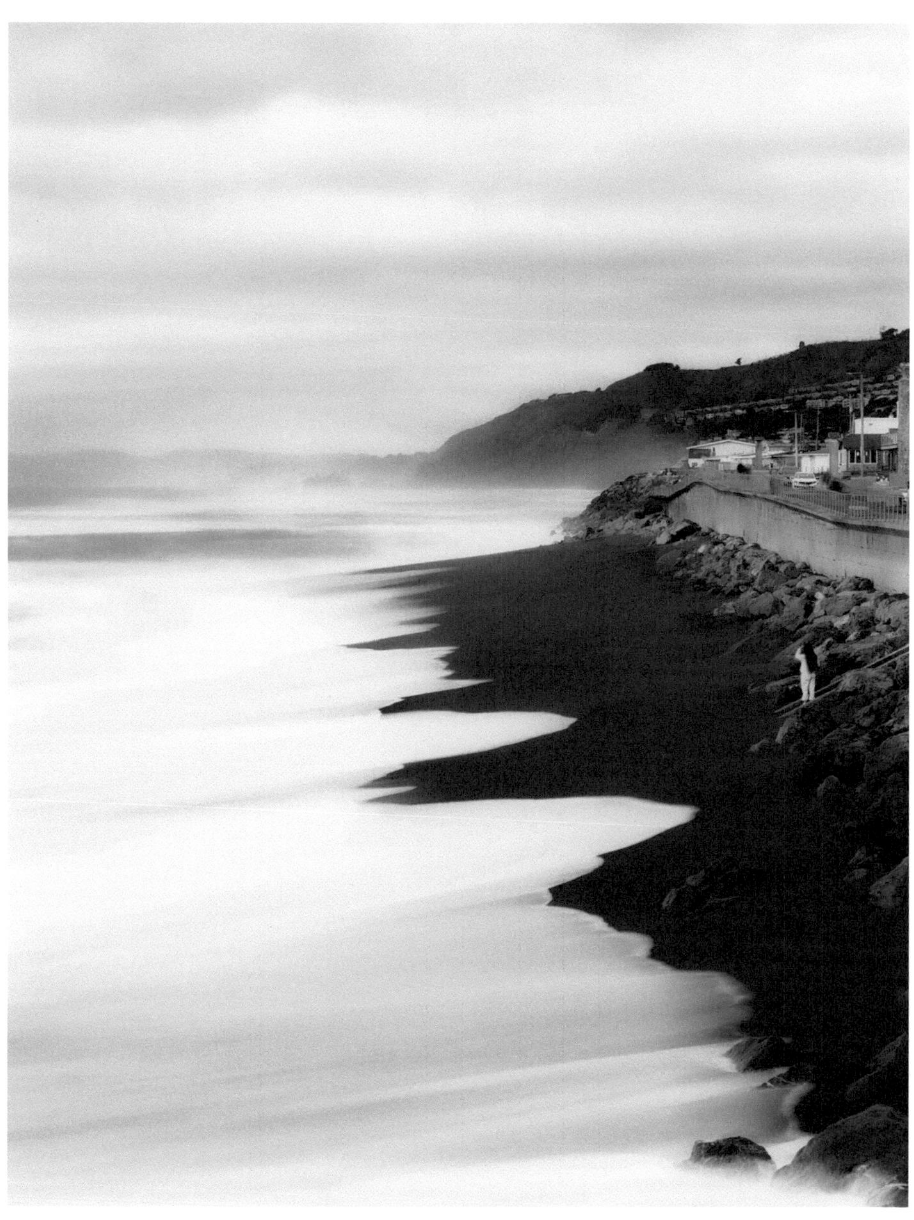

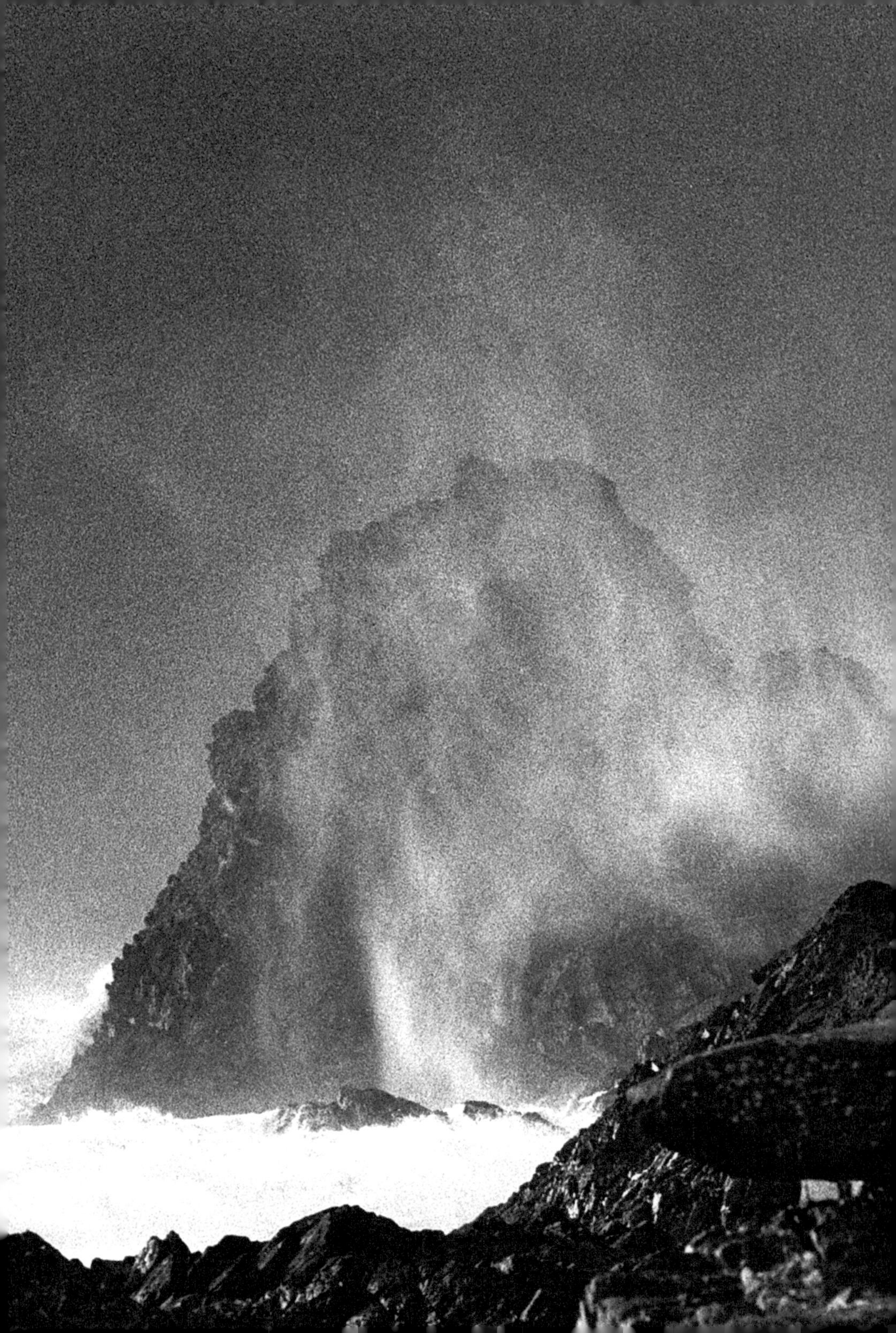

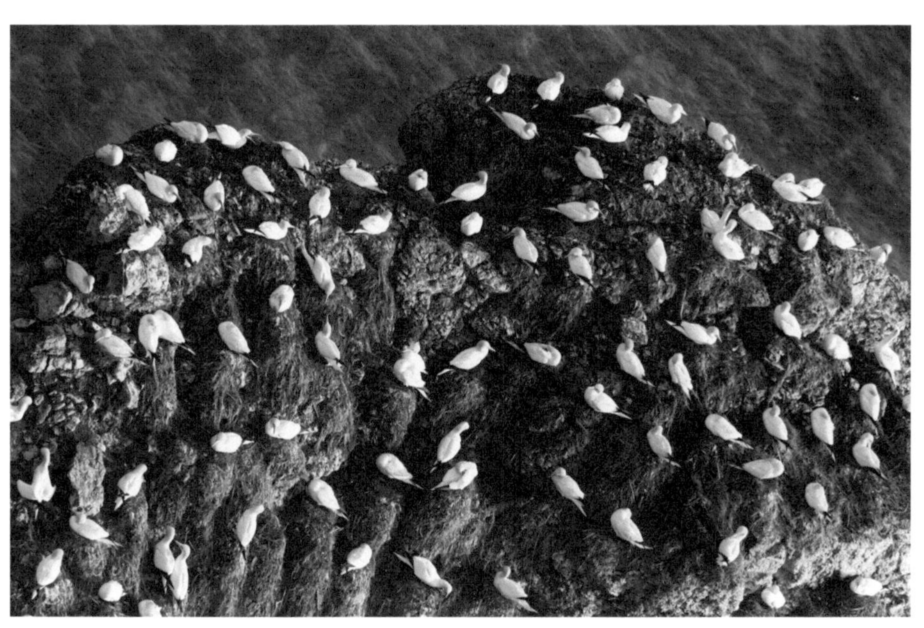

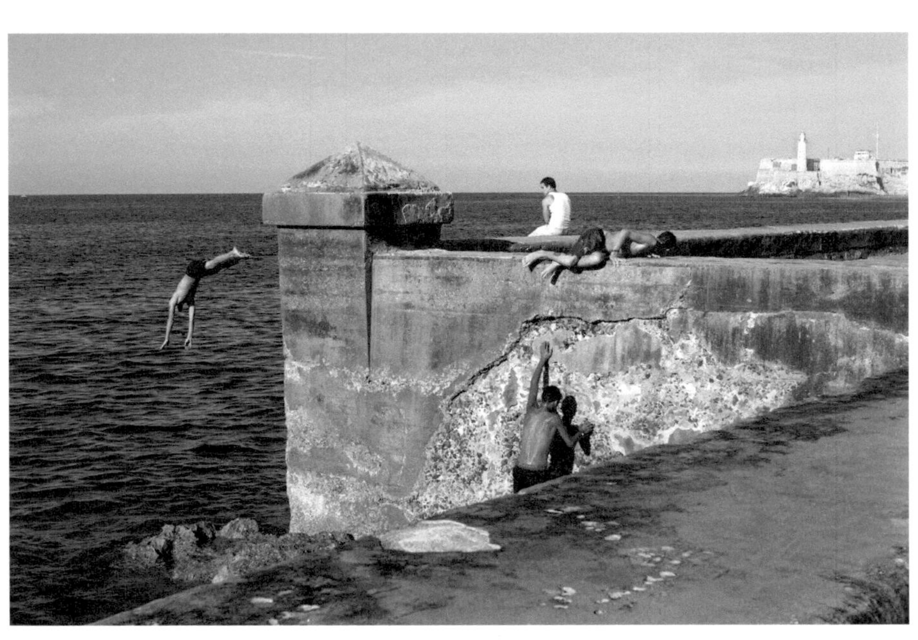

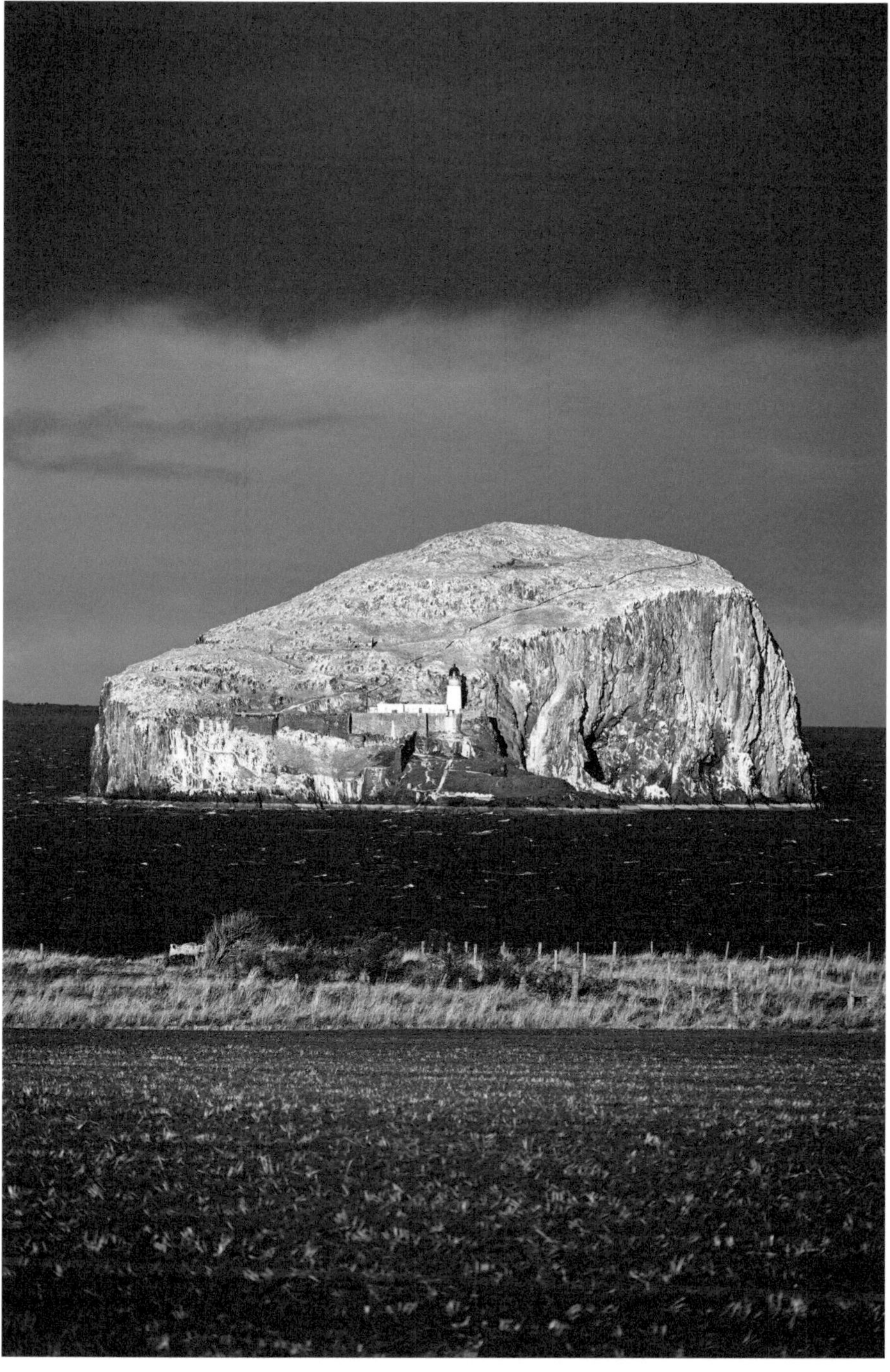

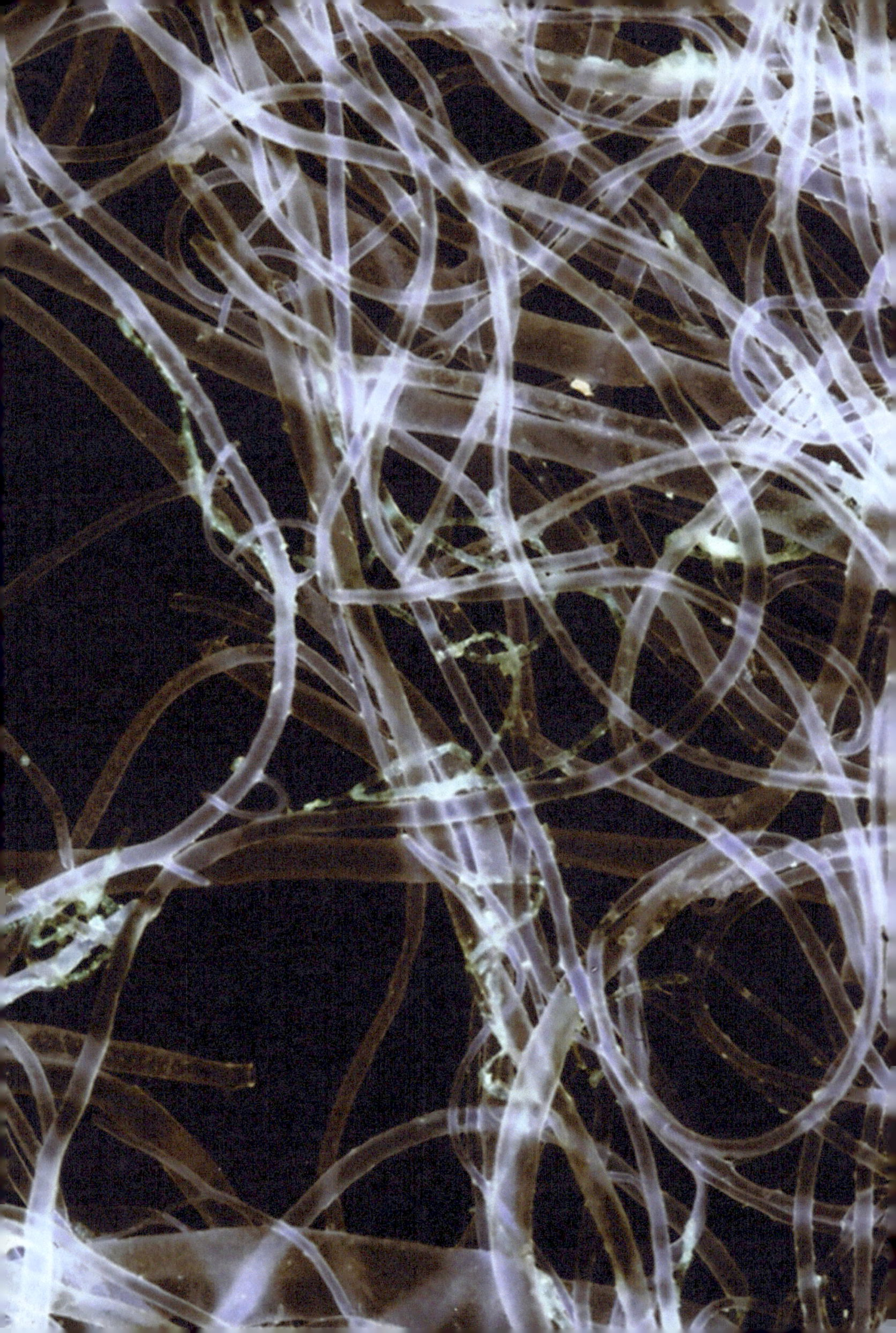

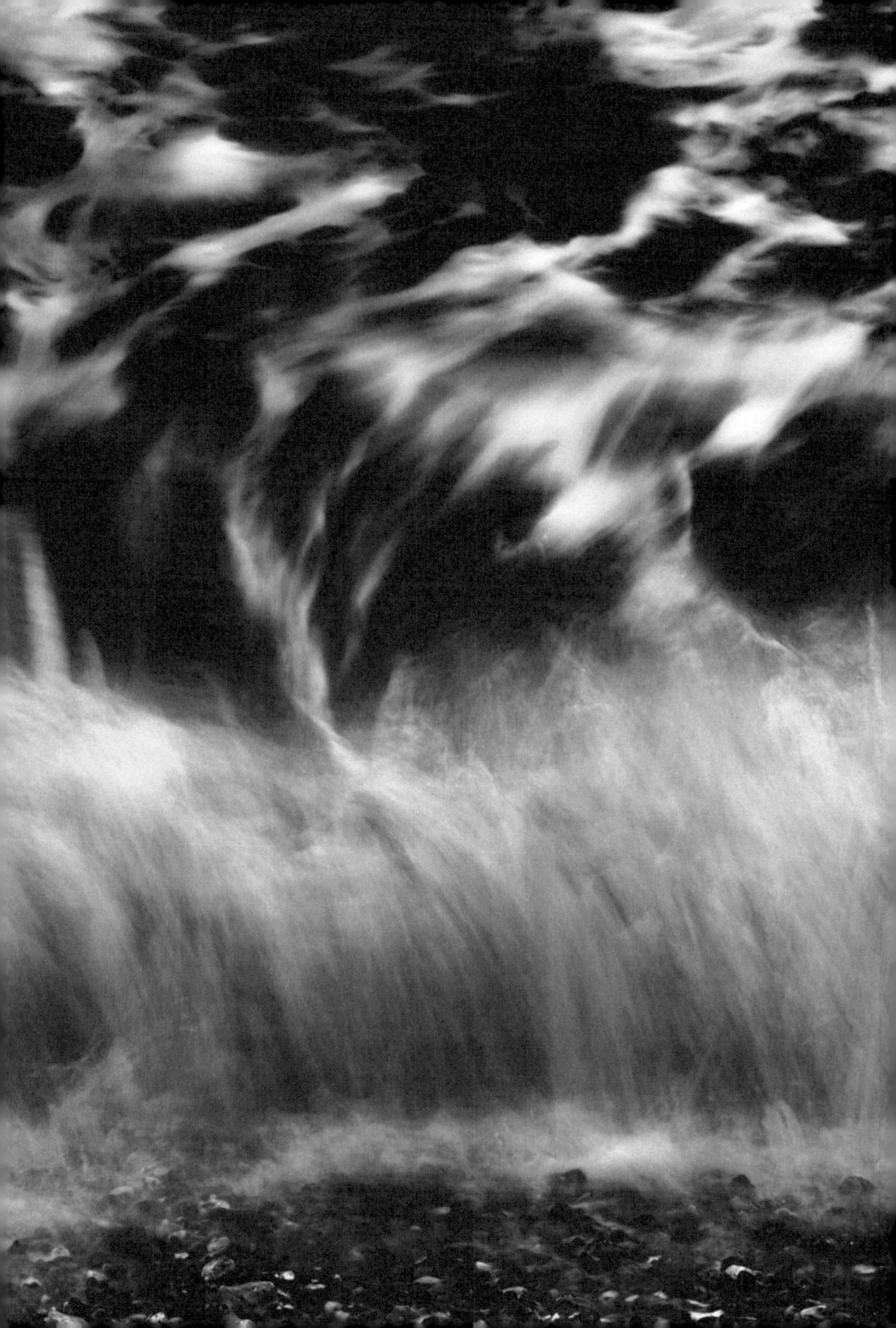

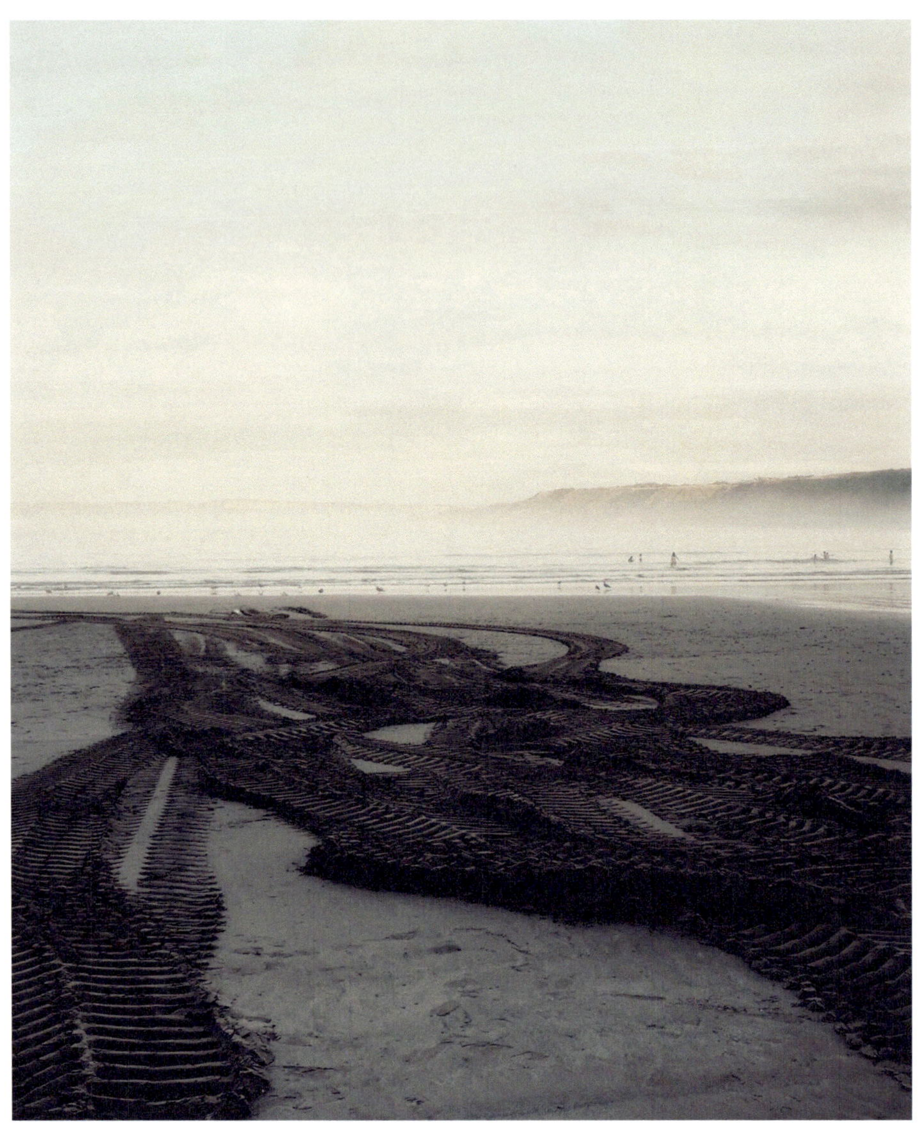

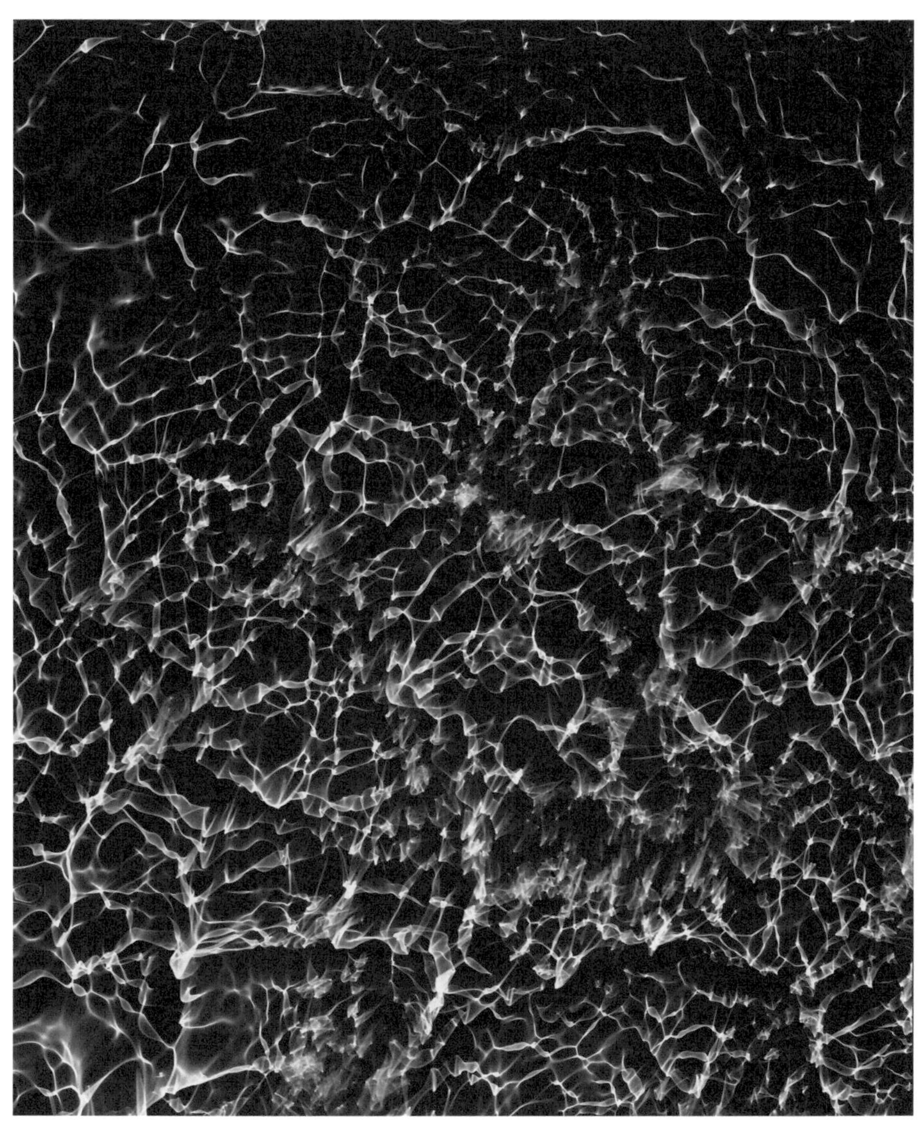

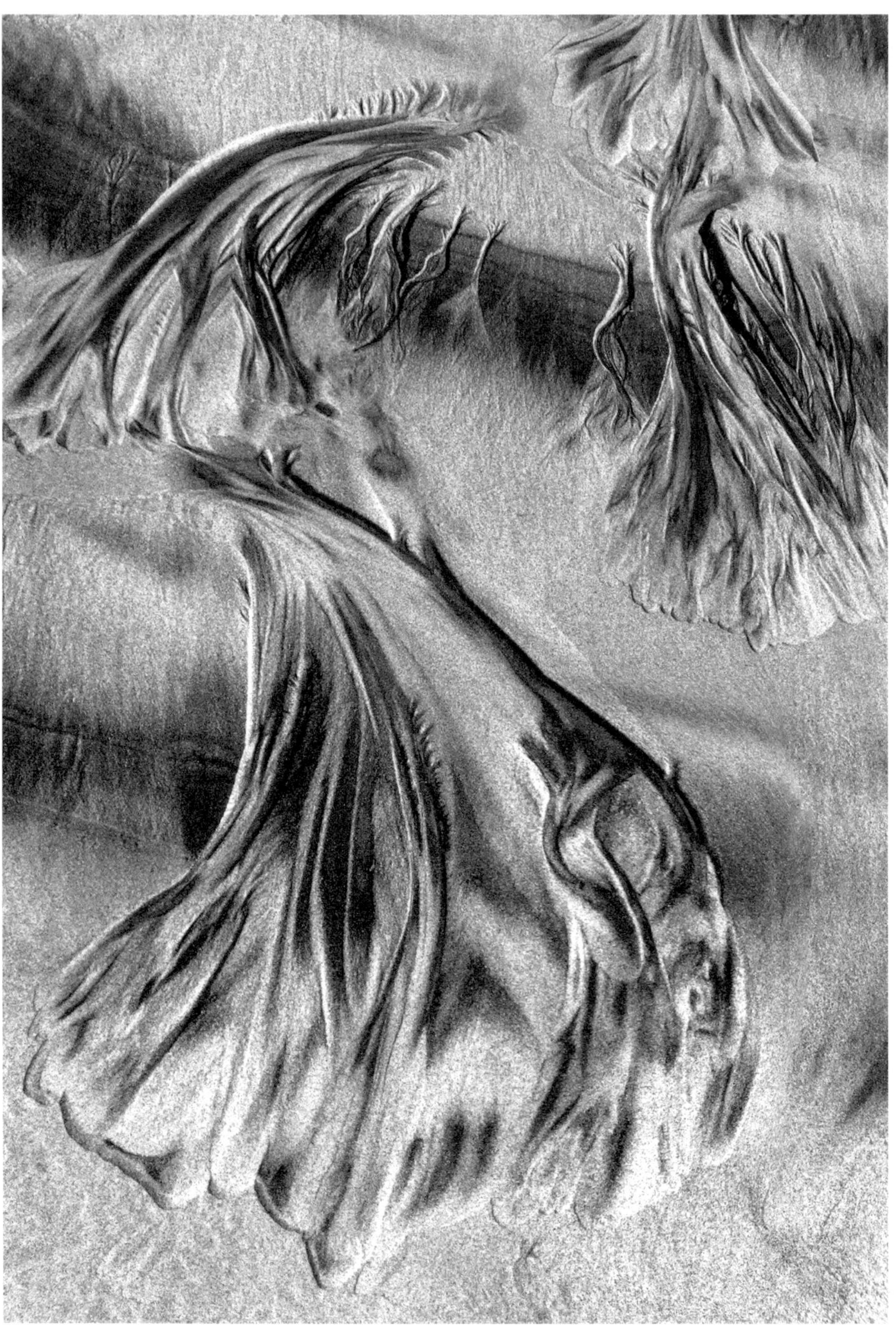

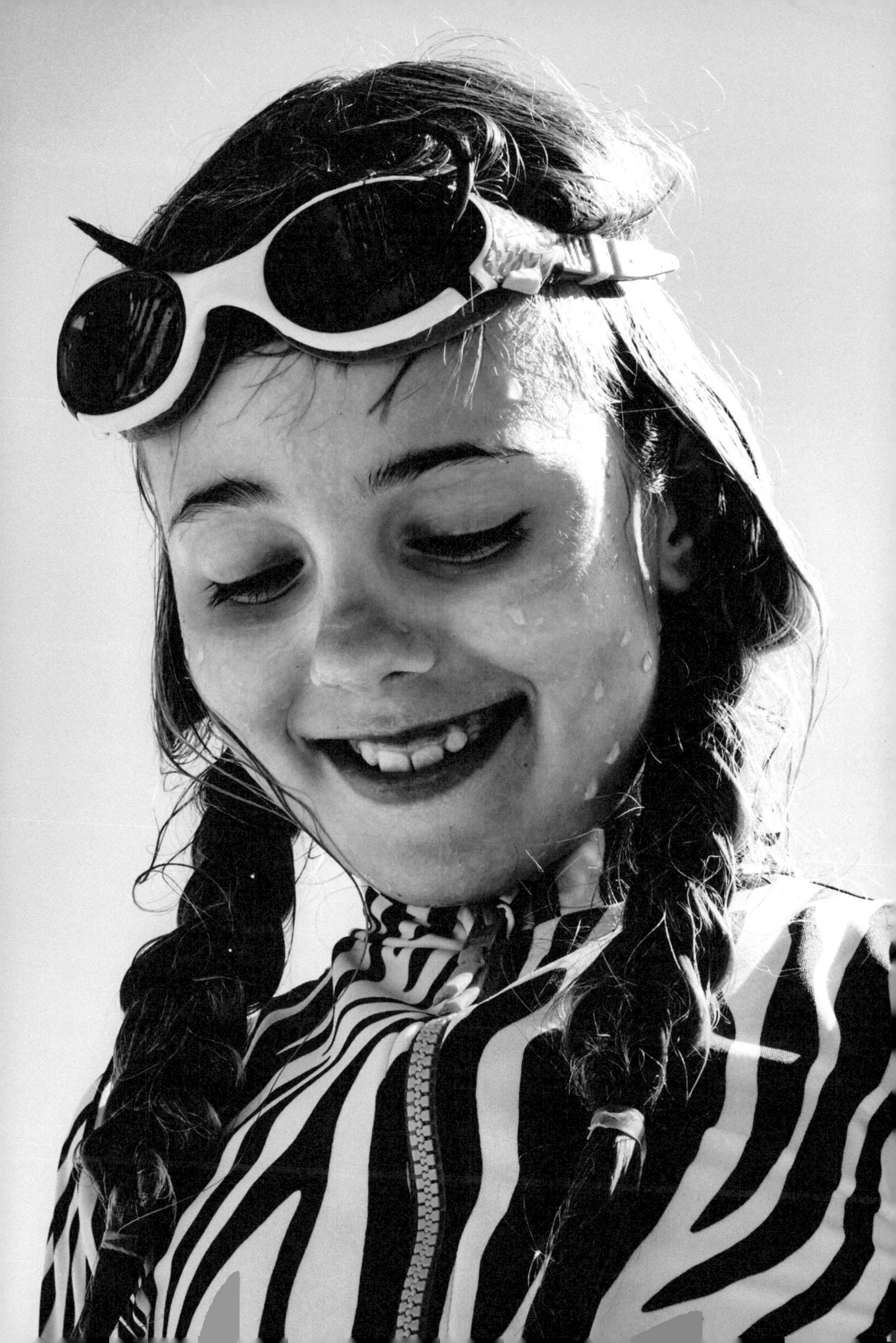

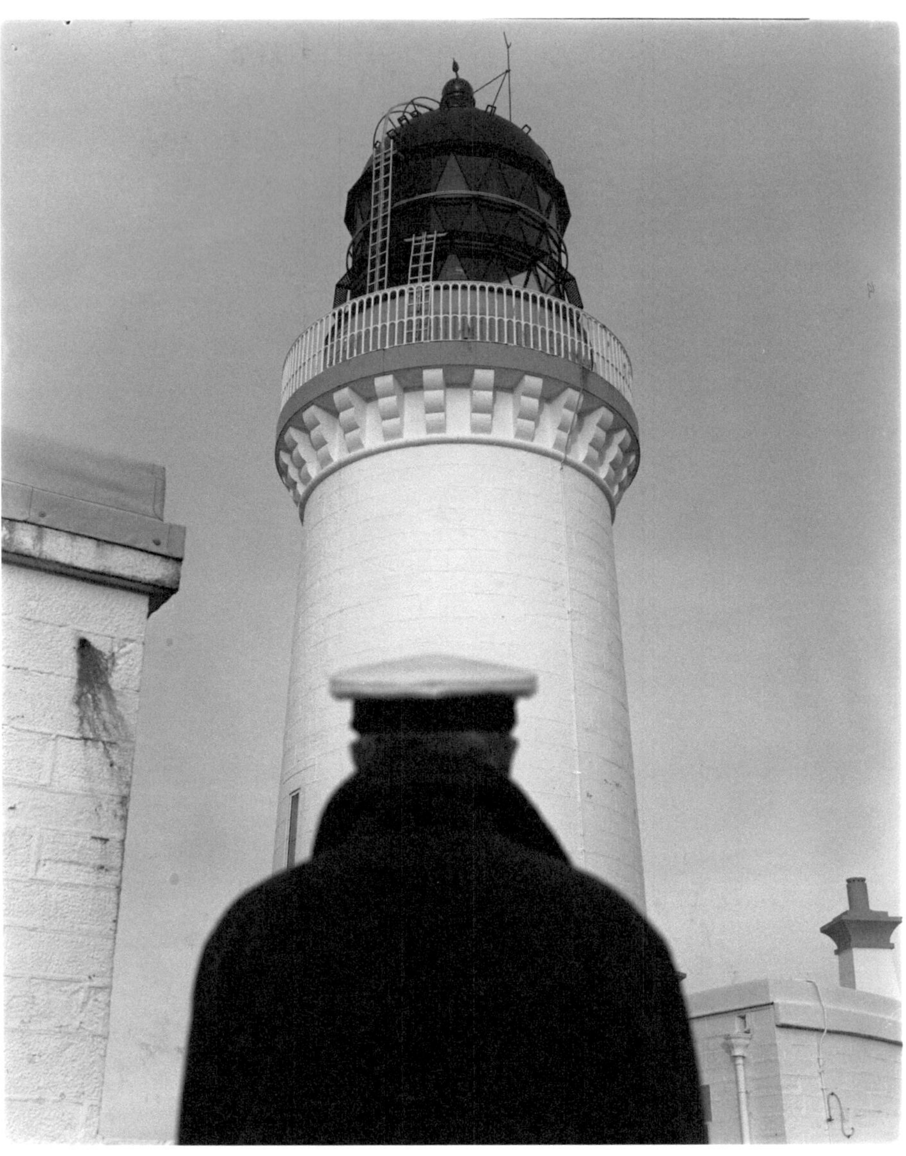

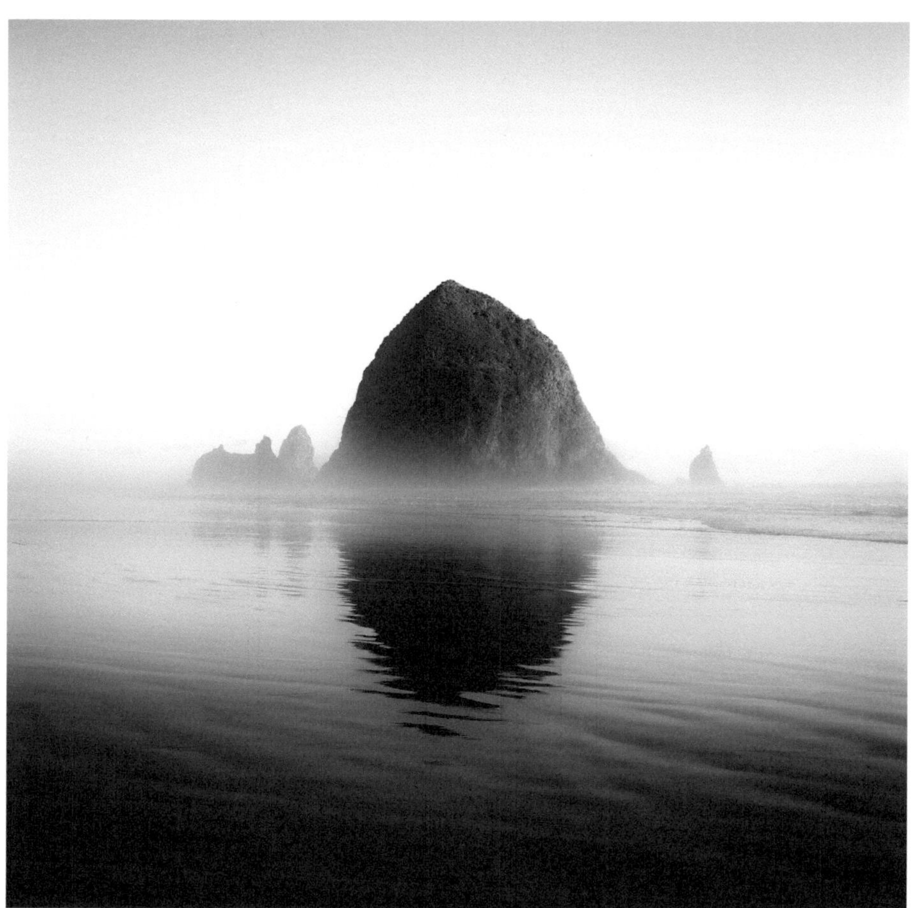

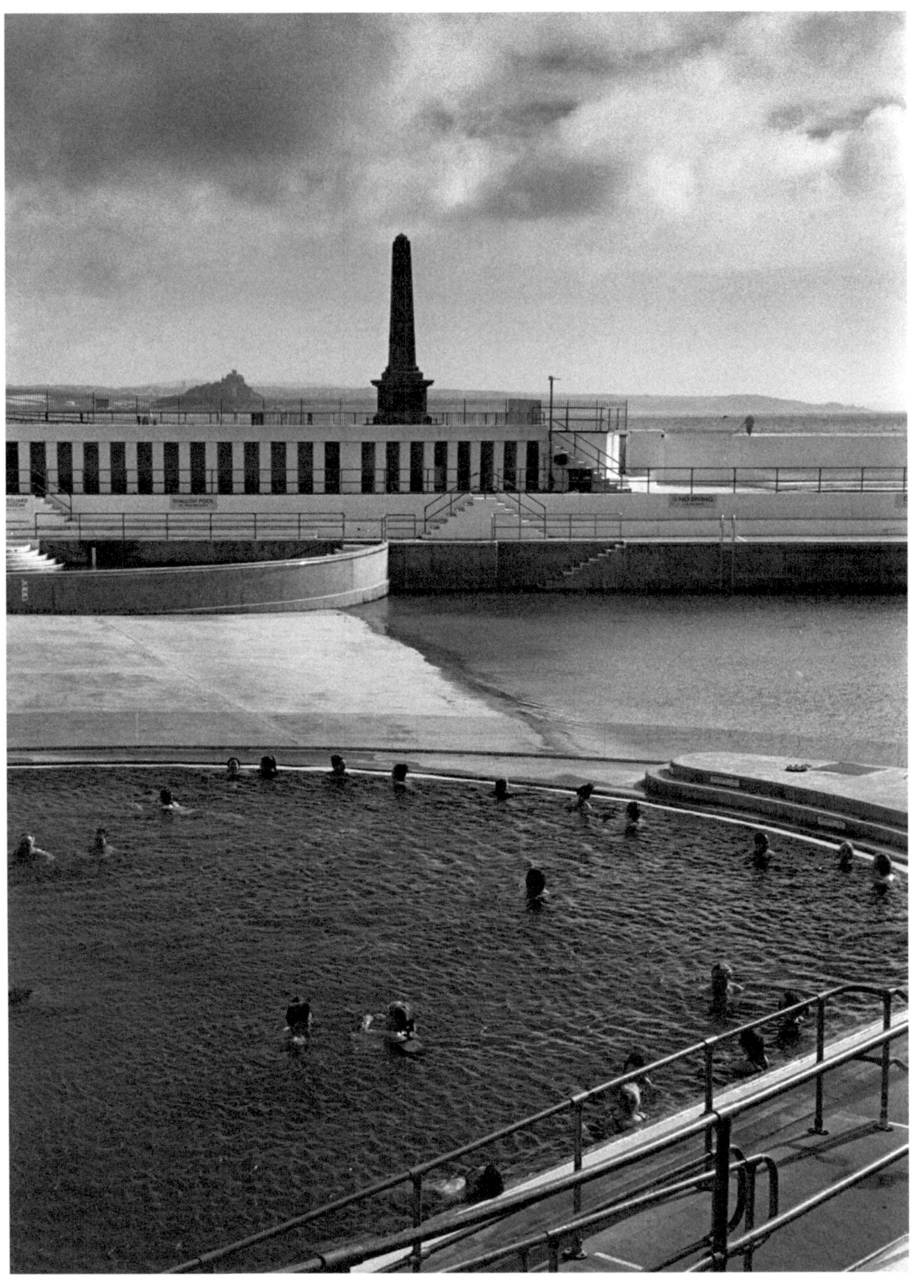
SHALLOW POOL
NO DIVING

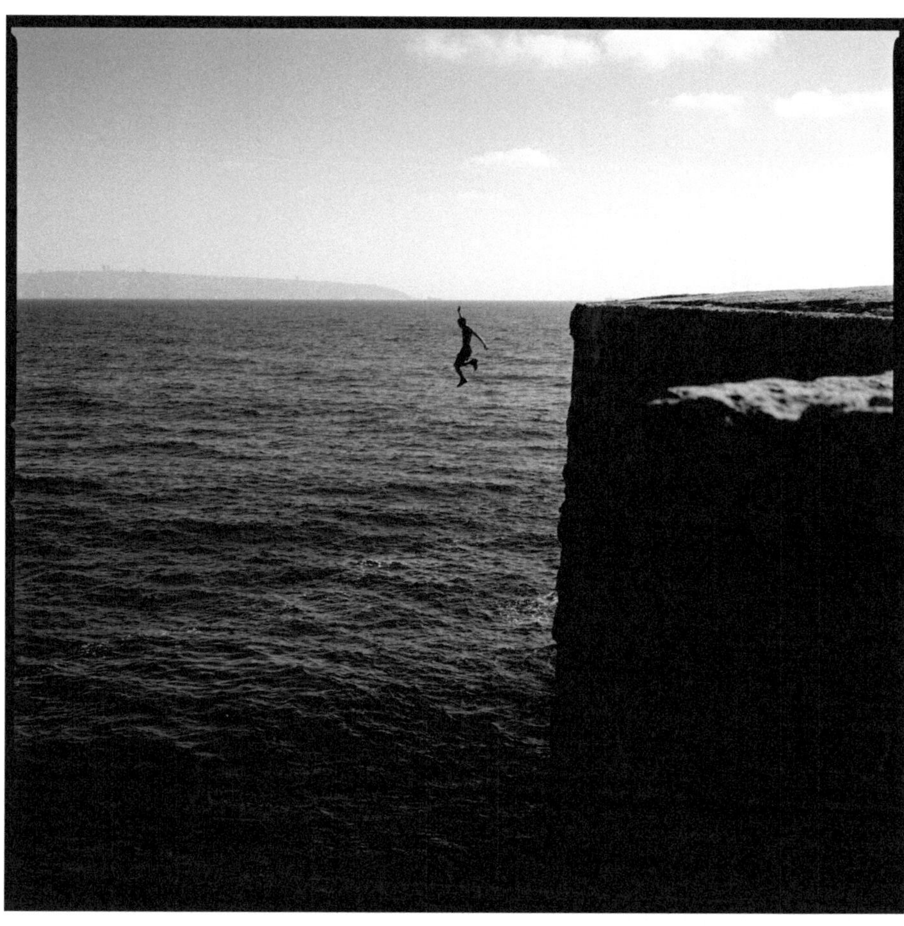

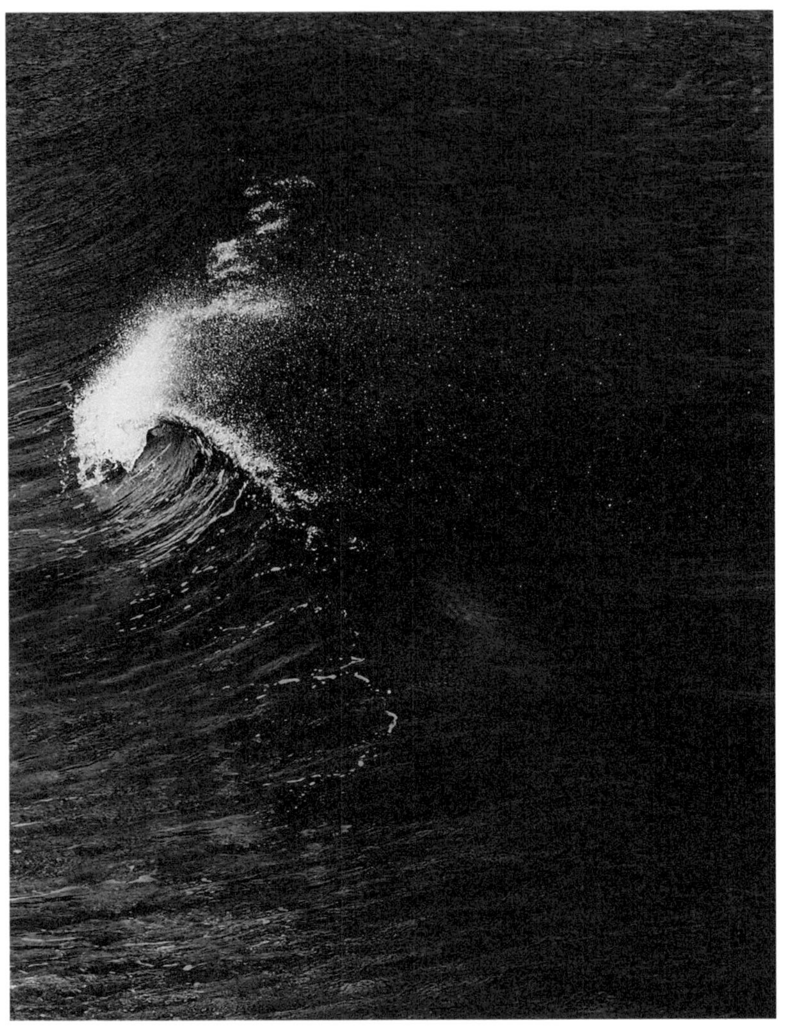

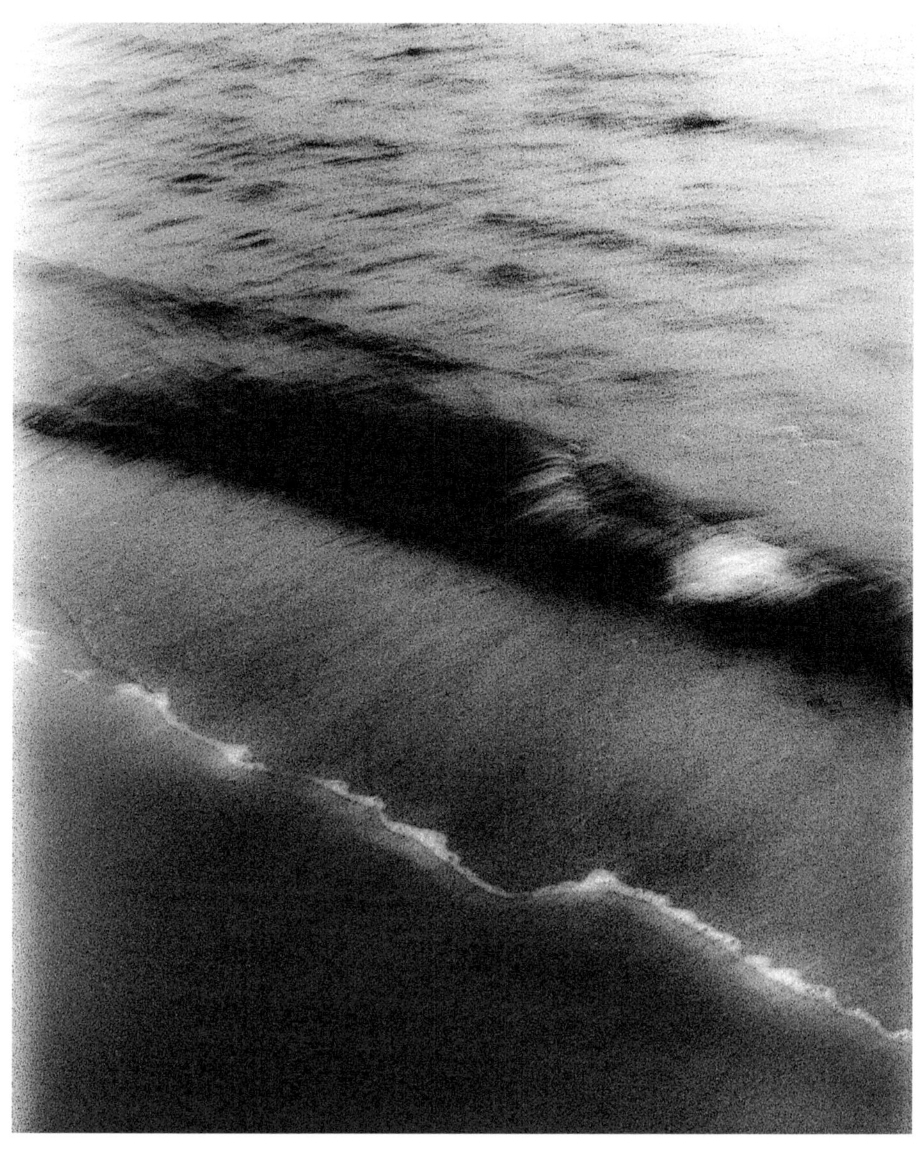

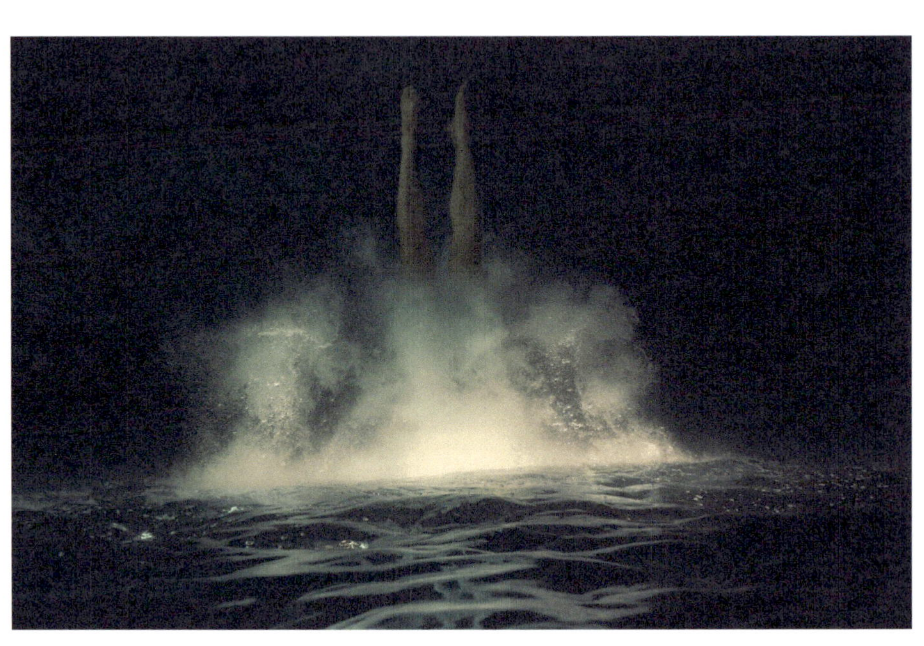

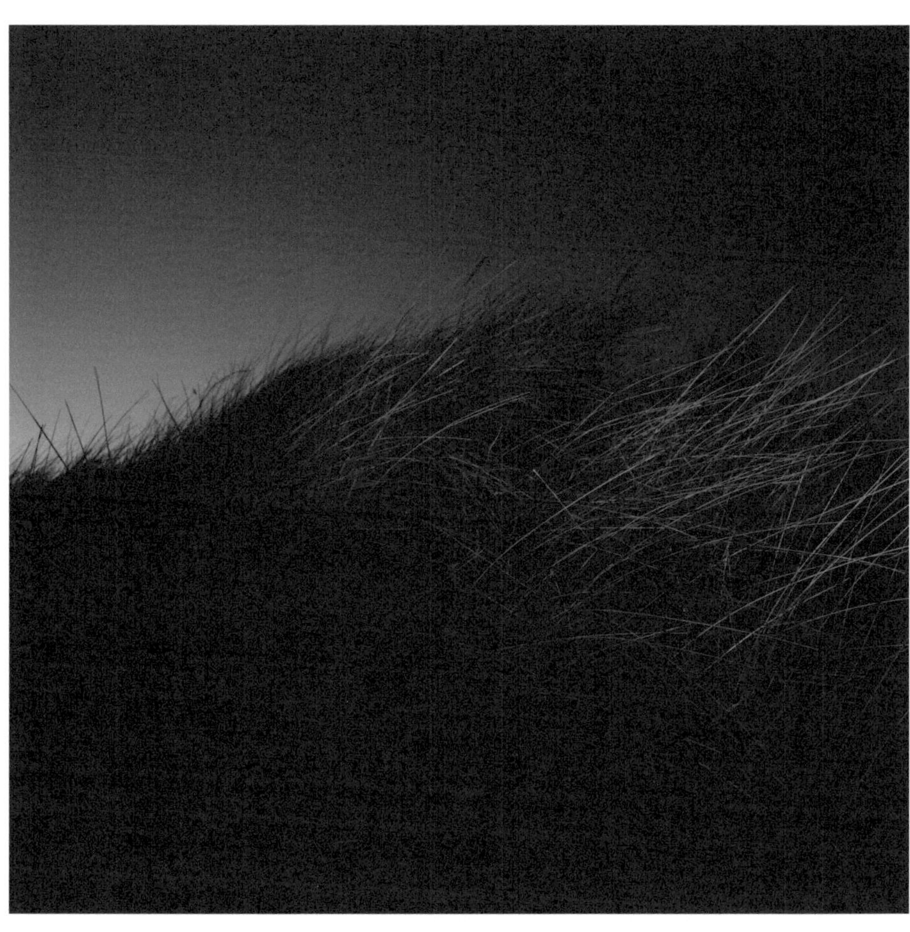

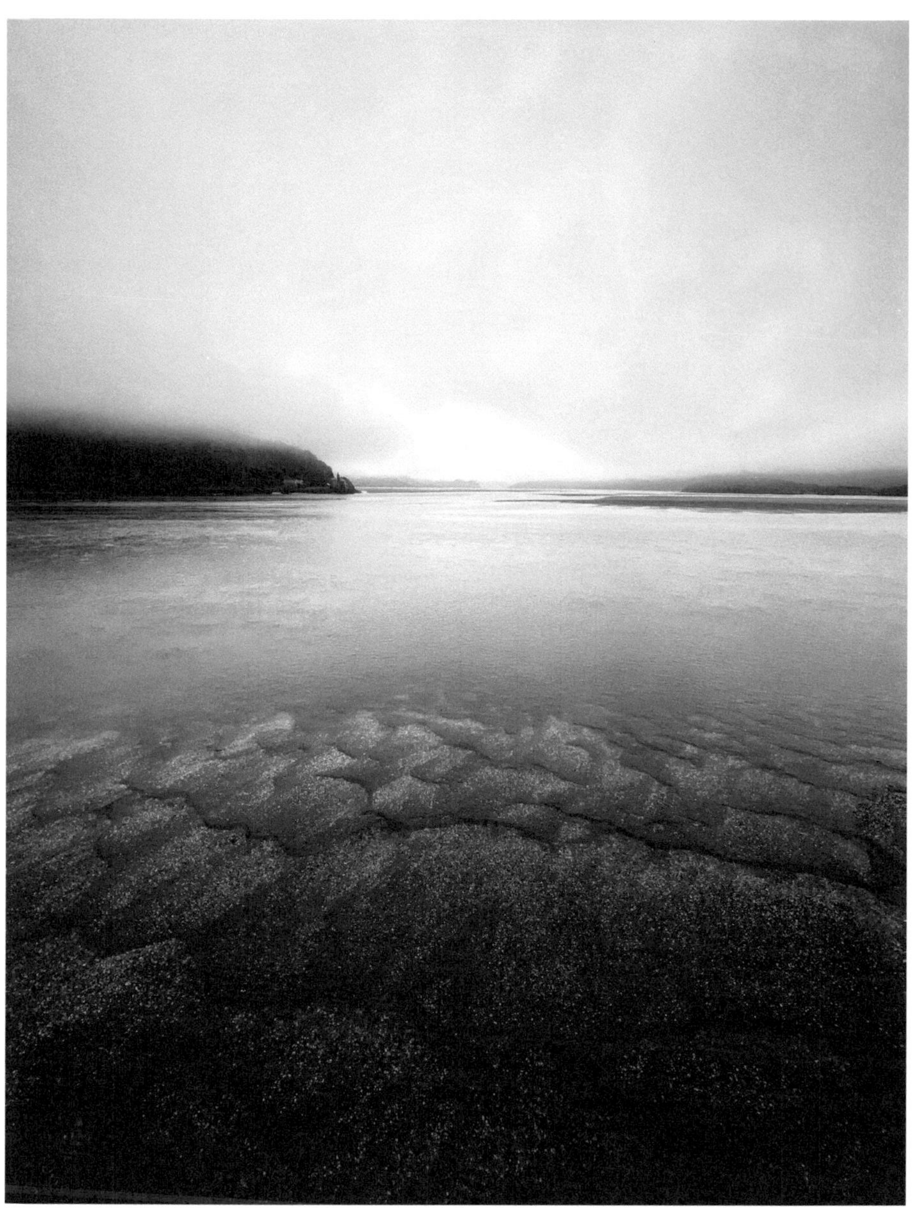

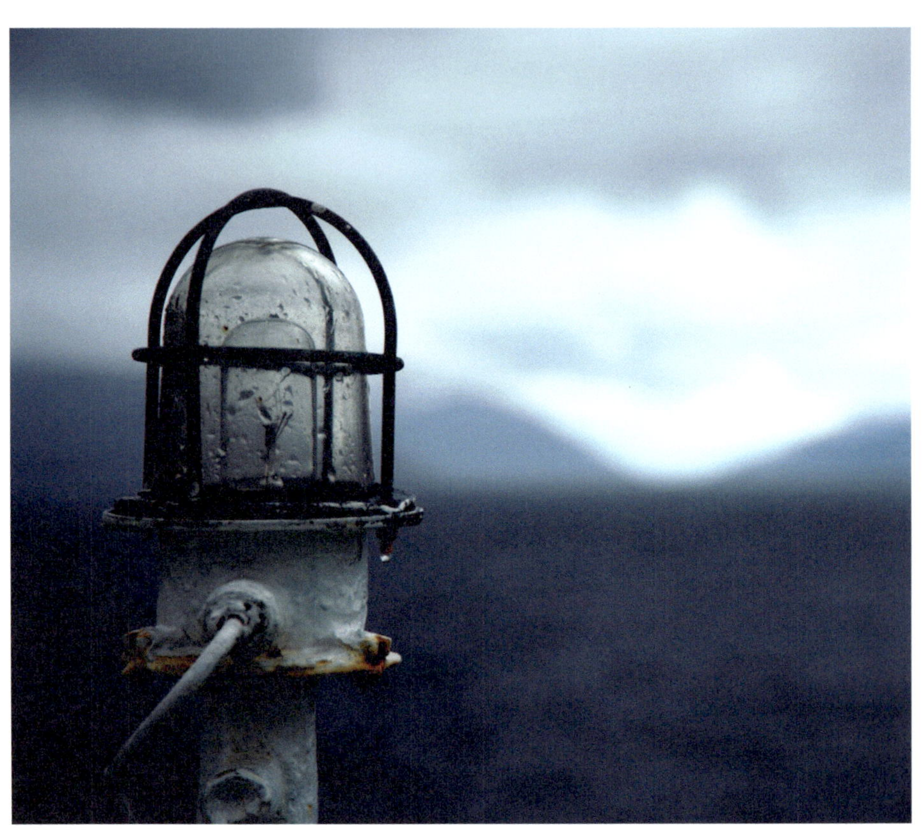

E221FFU001K
1140 mg 10:54

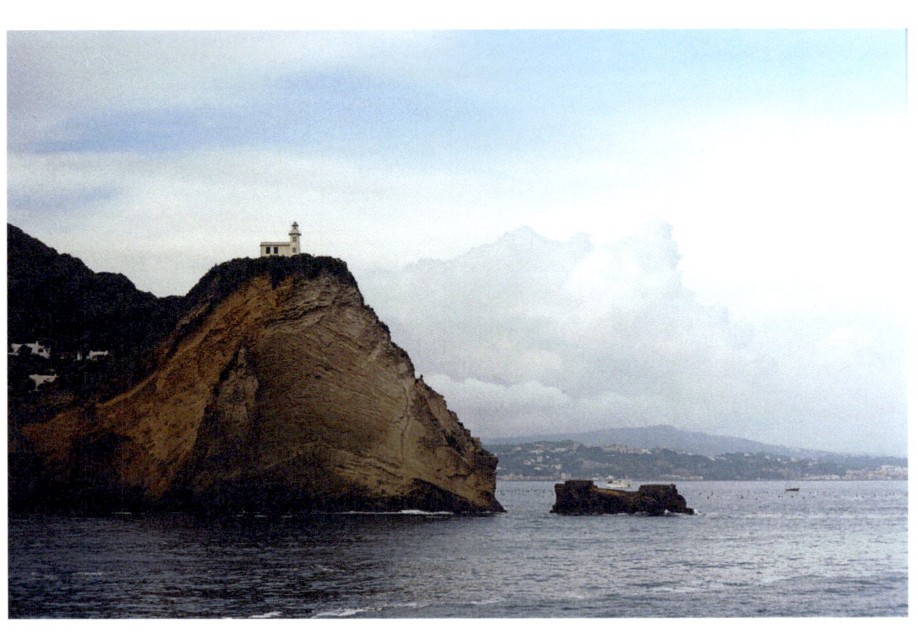

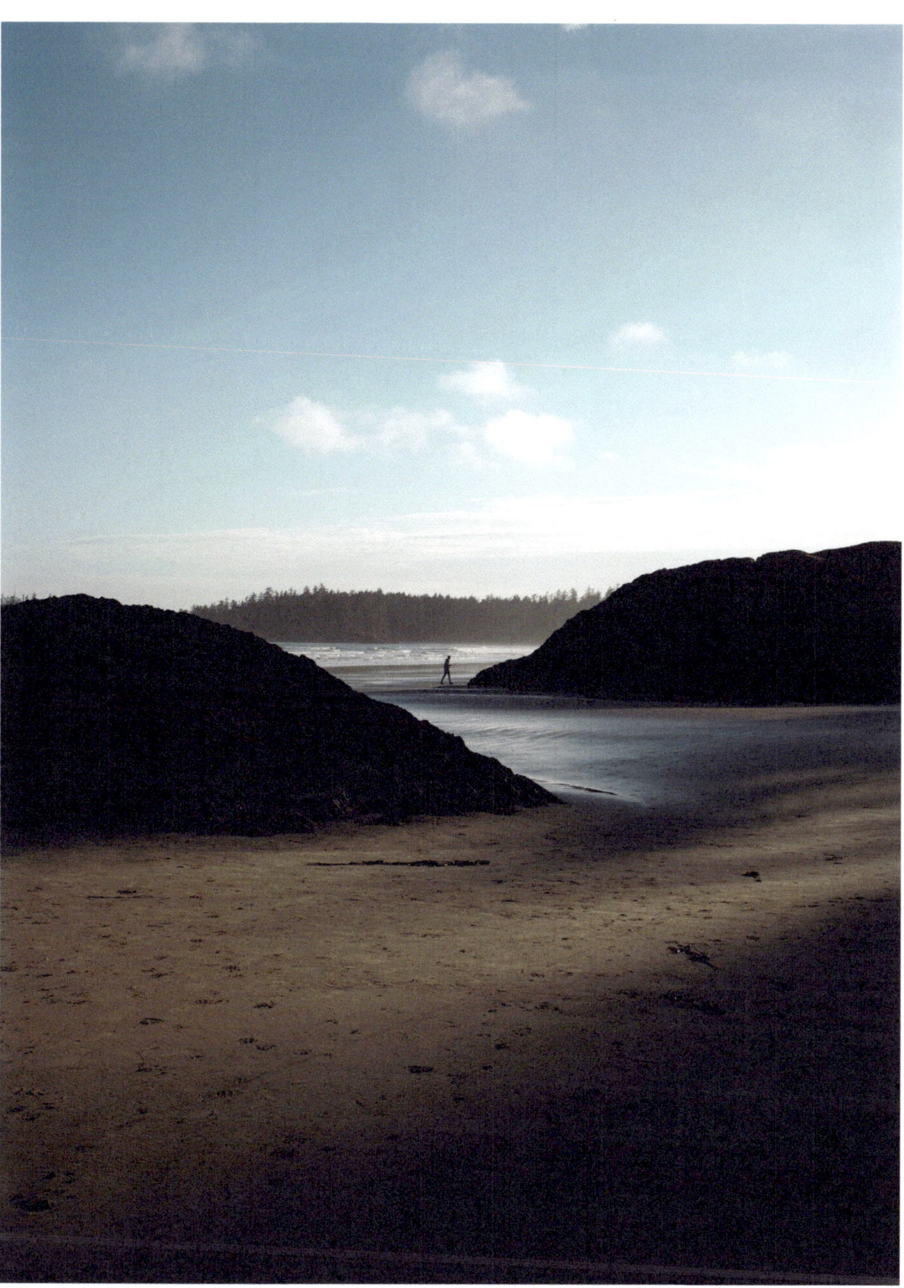

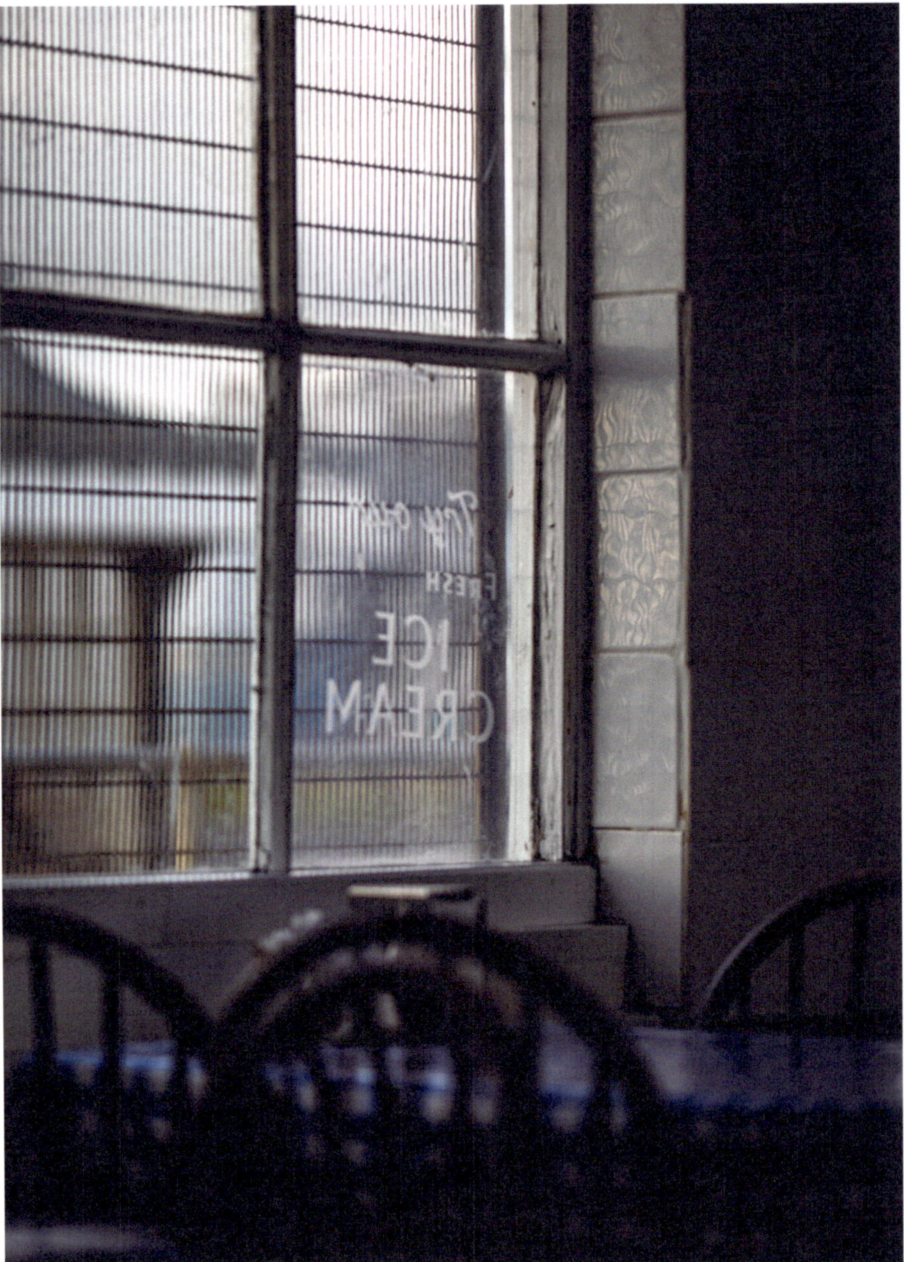
FRESH
ICE
CREAM

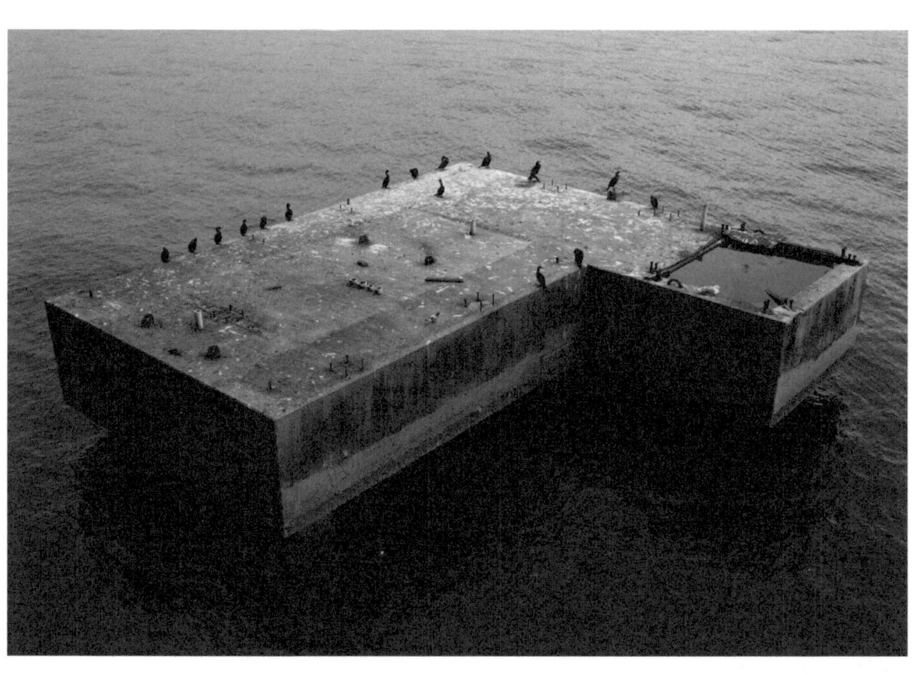

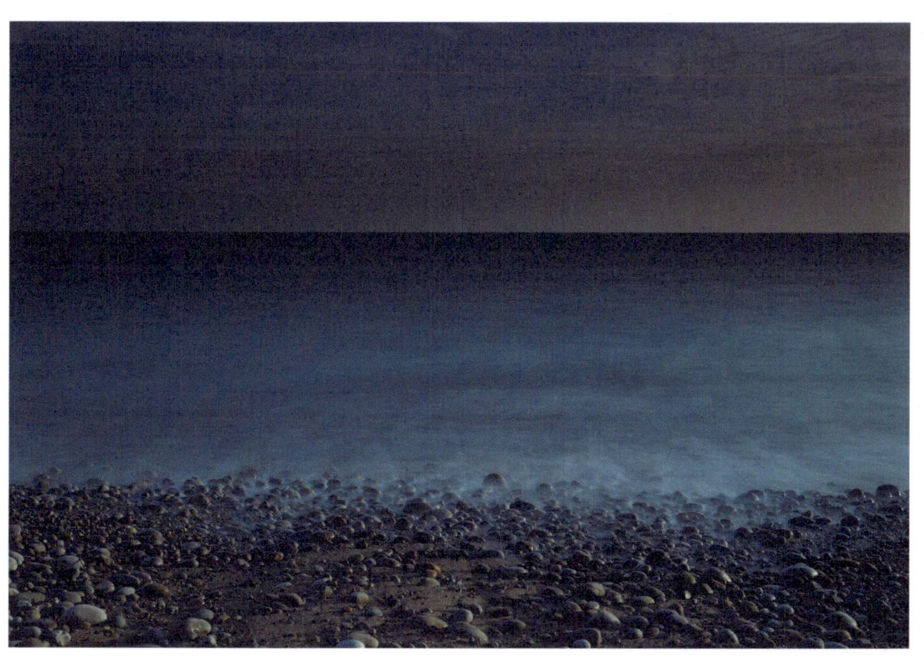

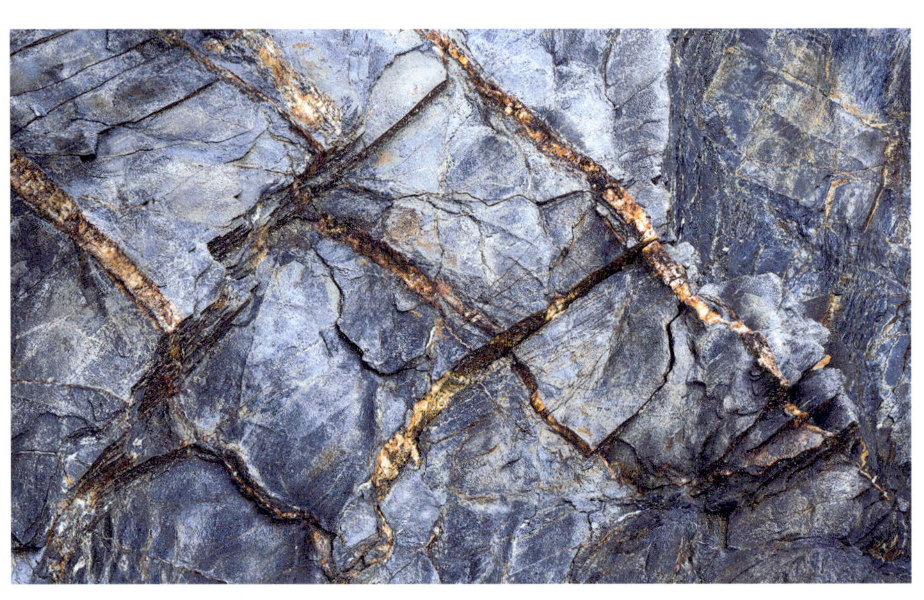

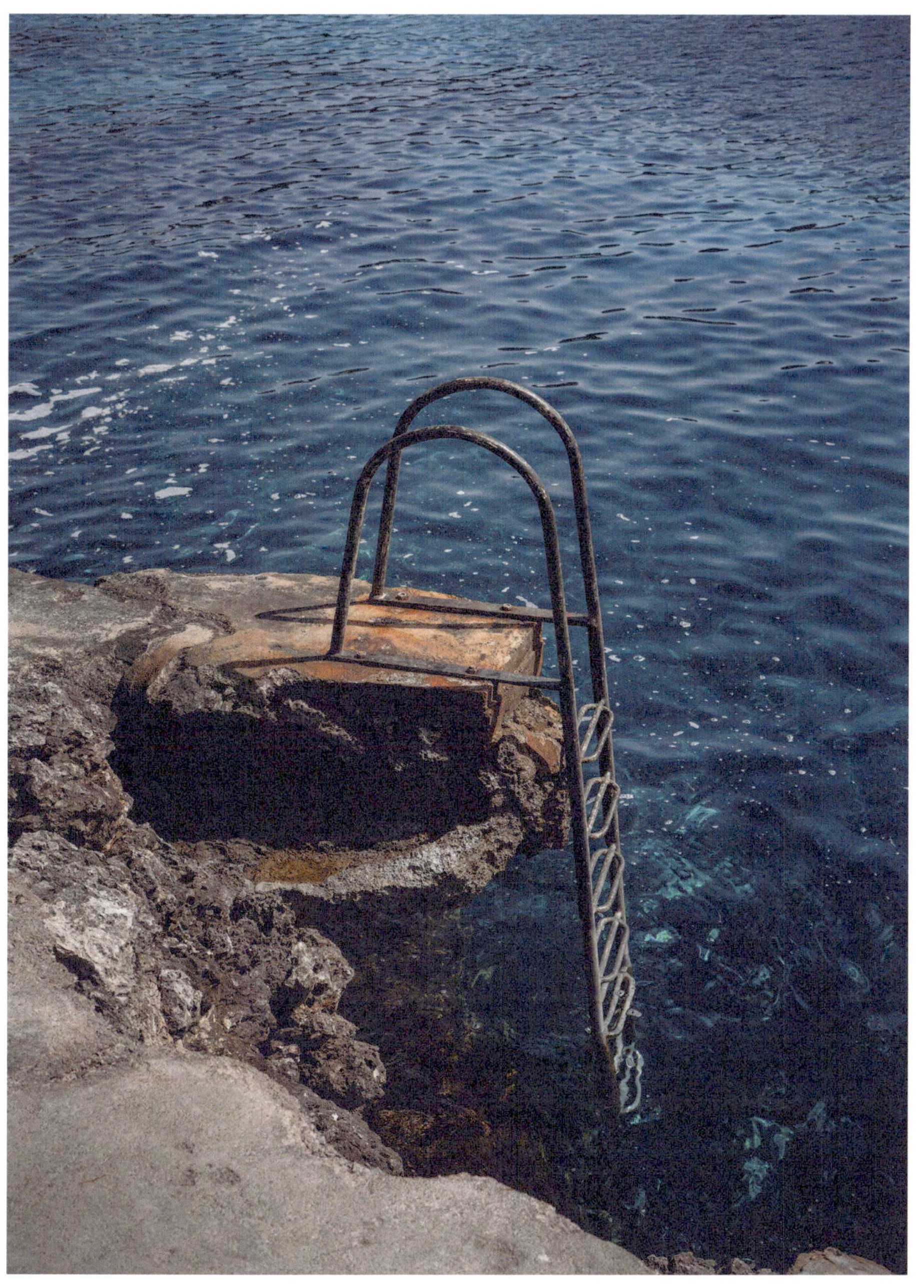

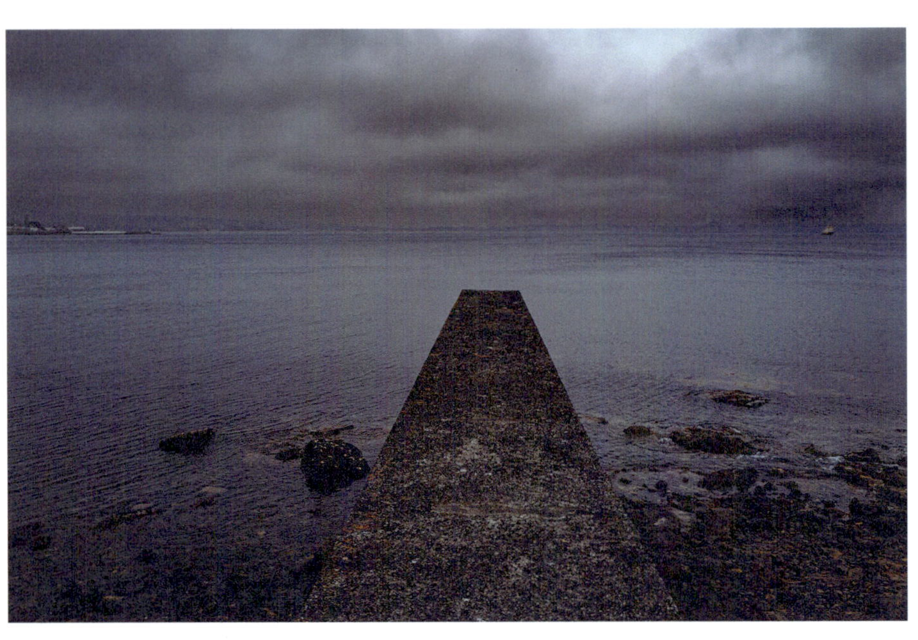

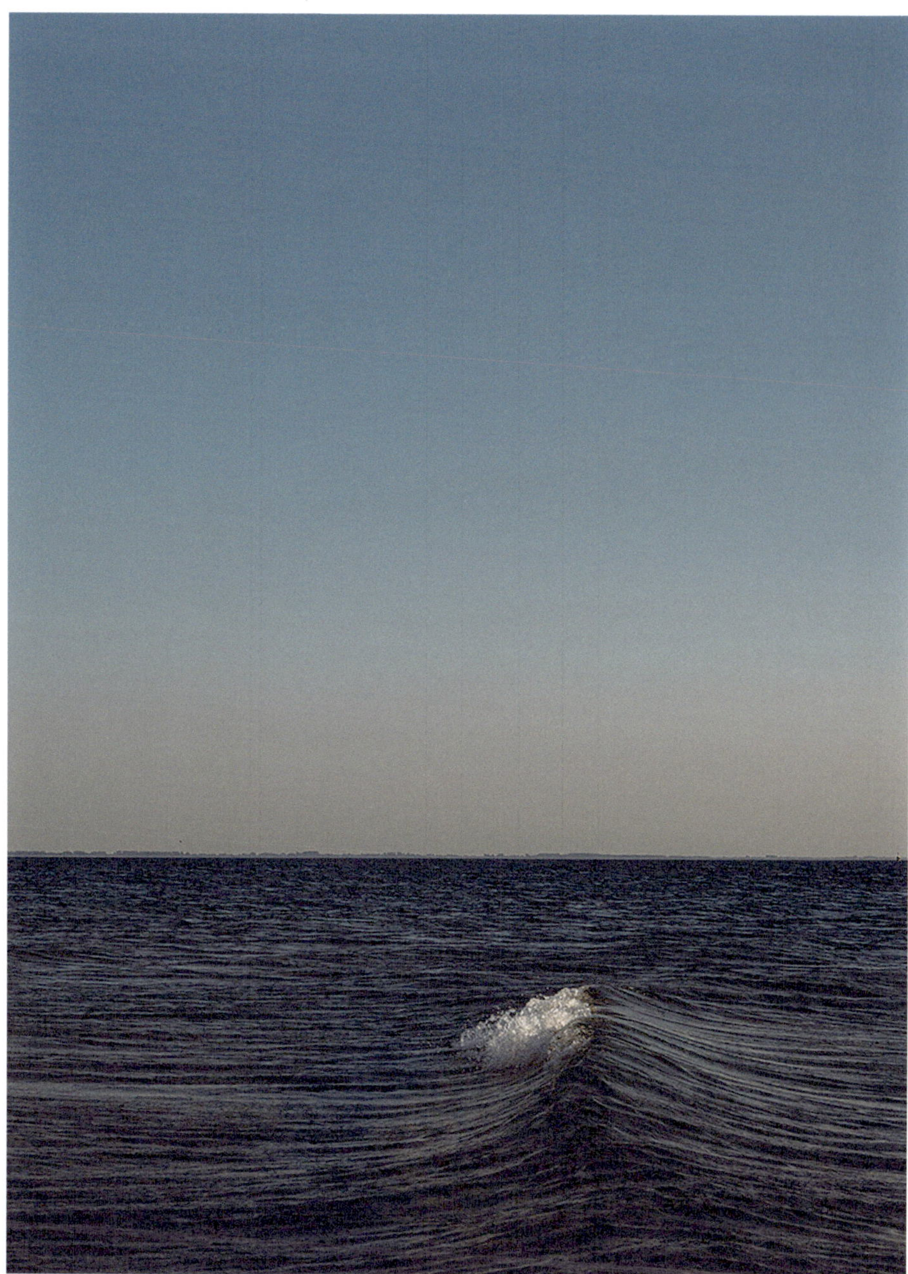

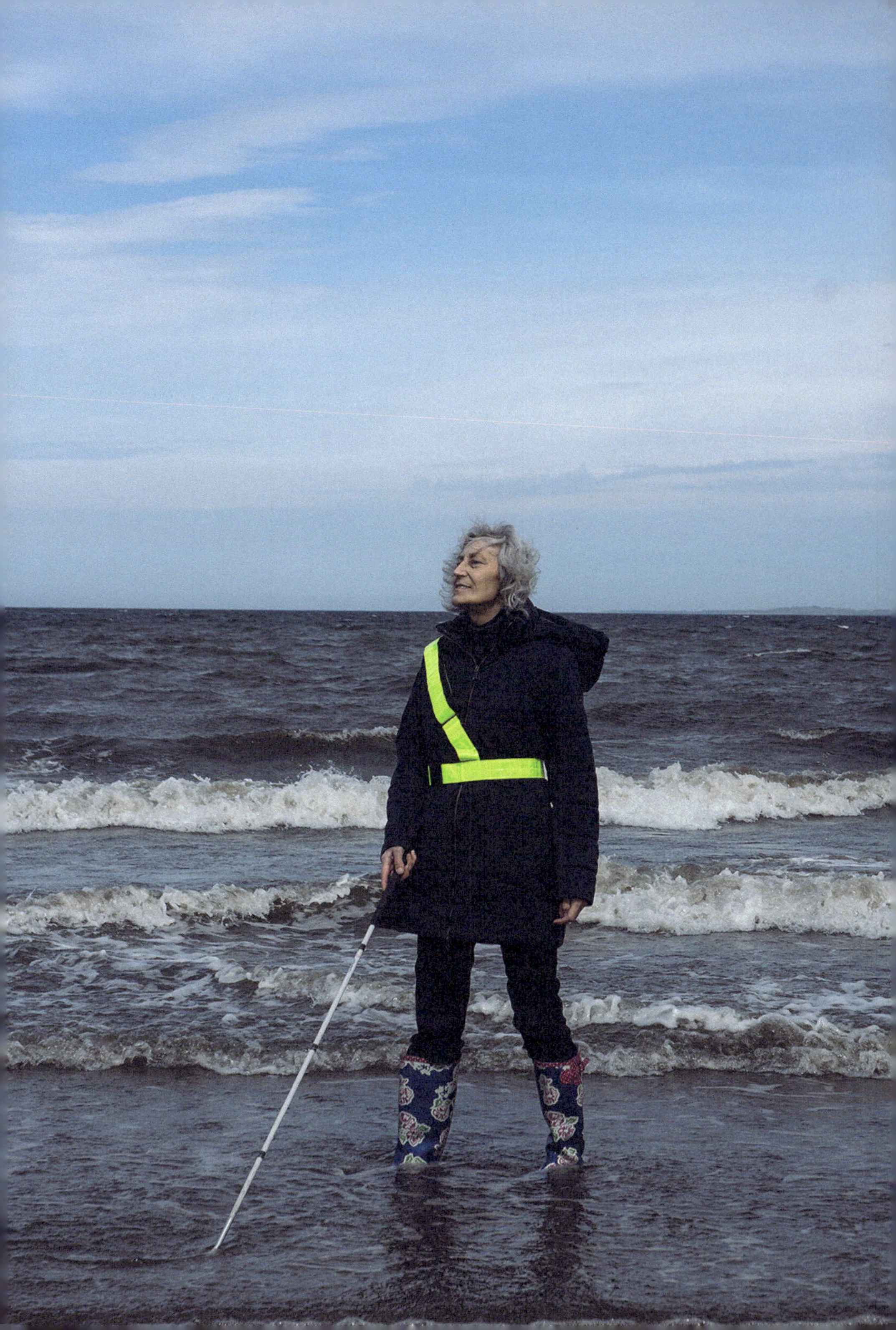

INDEX

Thank you to all the photographers who shared their work and have made this book possible.

We invite you to connect with these photographers and explore more of their work online.

Scan the QR code below or visit shutterhub.org.uk/shutter-hub-editions-to-the-sea

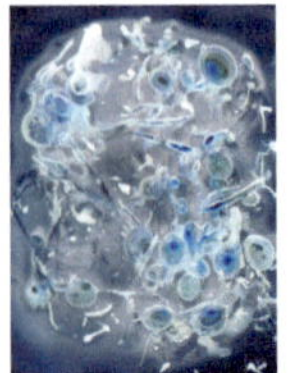
Anna Sellen

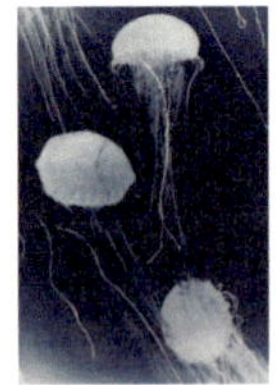
Jo Stapleton

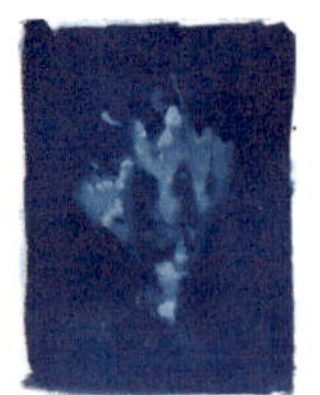
Sally Gunnett

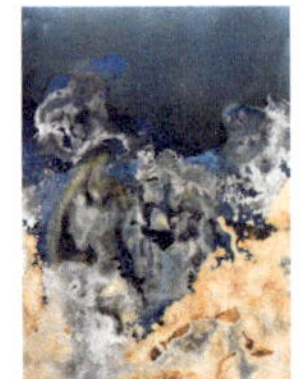
Aindreas Scholz

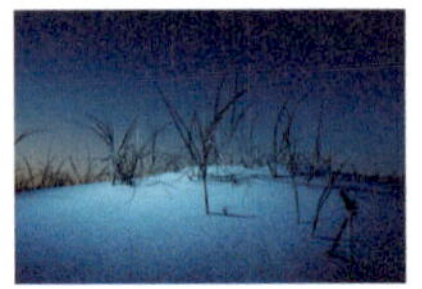
Dominik Scharf

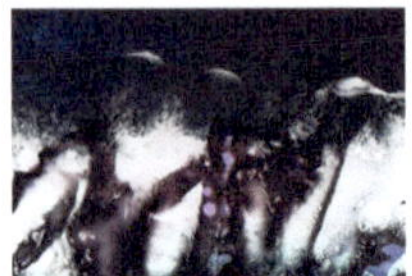
Tee Chandler

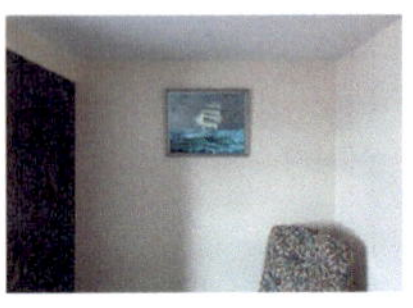
Paul Walsh

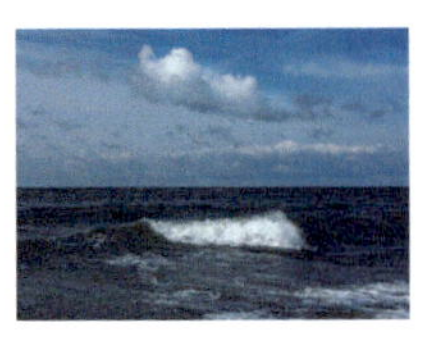
Dineke Versluis

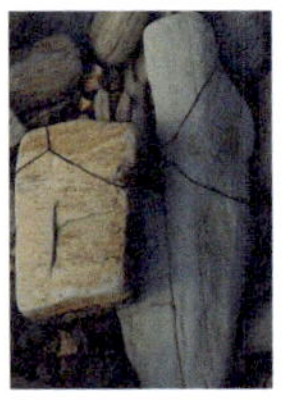
Ann Russell

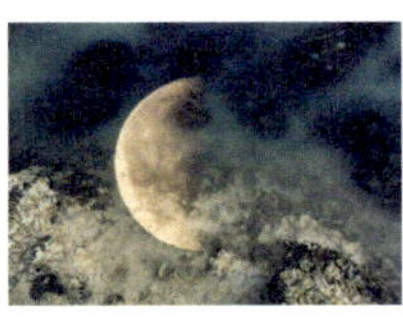
Carolyn Lefley

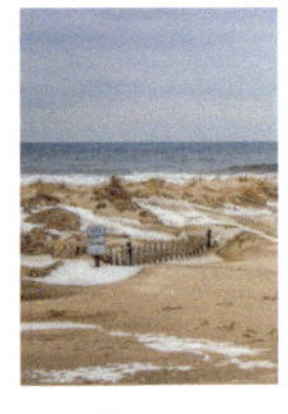
Vin Sharma

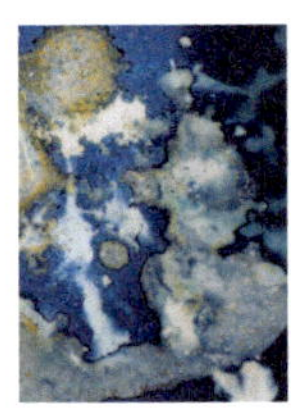
Anne Campbell

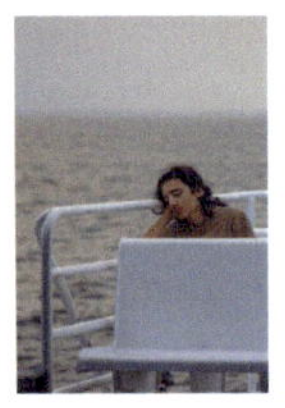
Vin Sharma

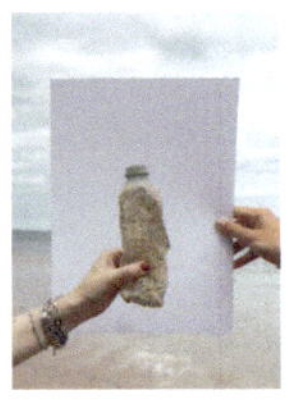
Clair Robins

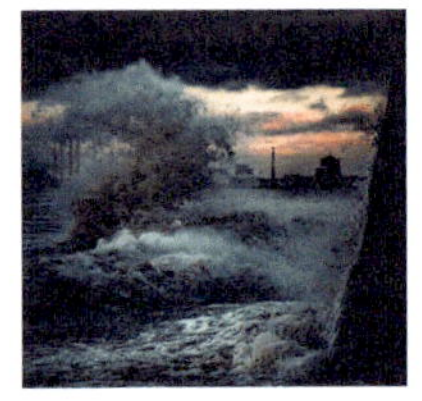
Natalie Persoglio

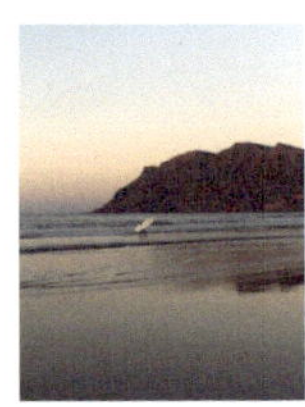
Altcada

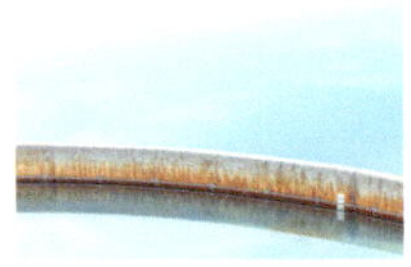
Duncan Petrie

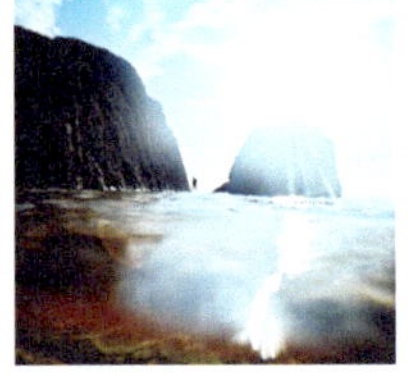
Wendy Aldiss

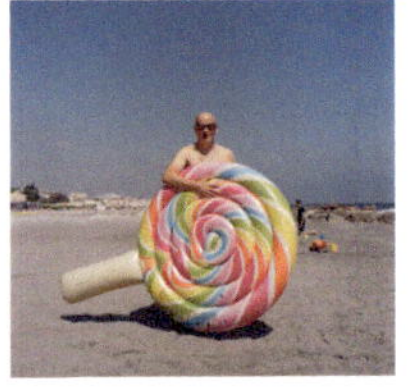
Paola Leonardi

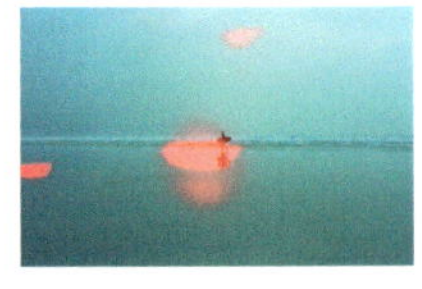
Laurence Donoghue

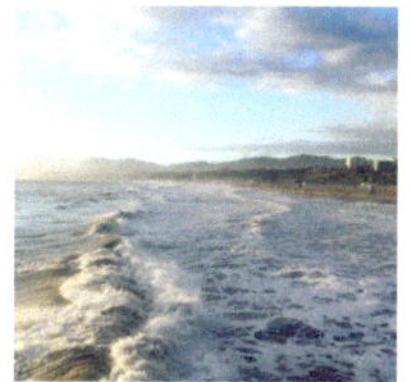

Bettina Stammen

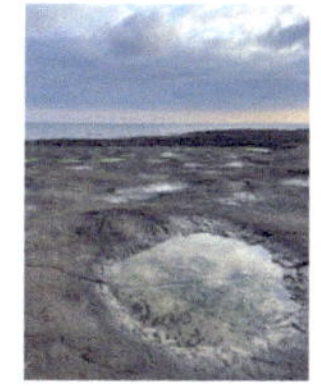

Sarah Callow

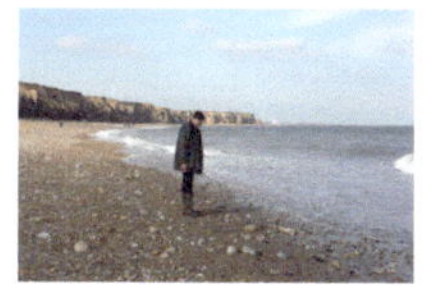

Rachel Manley

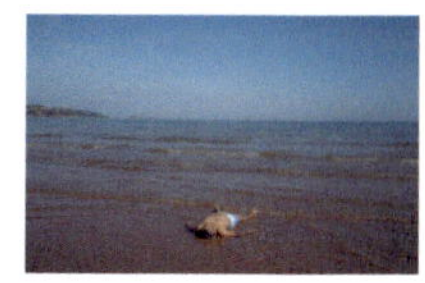

Kim Aldis

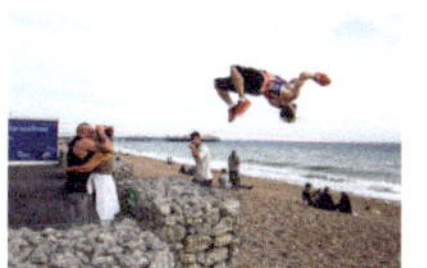

Darren Lehane

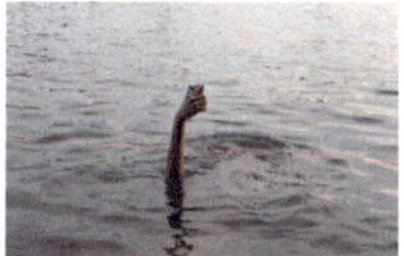

Lisa Achammer

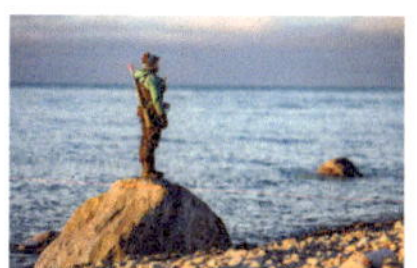

Laura Allen Noel

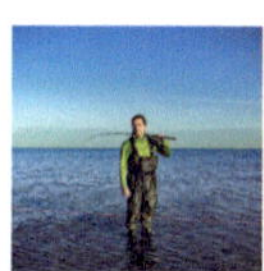

Trish Crawford

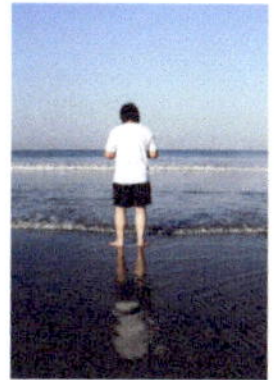

Patricia Belson

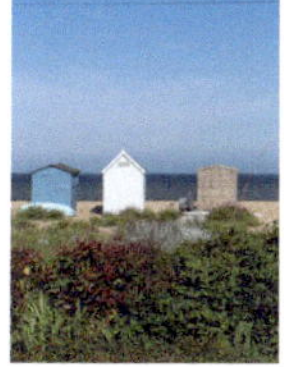

James Berrington

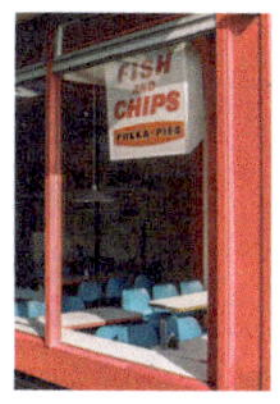

Poppy French

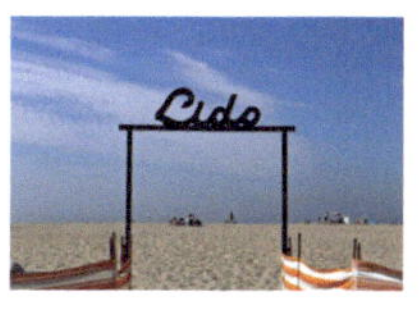

Juliet Ferguson

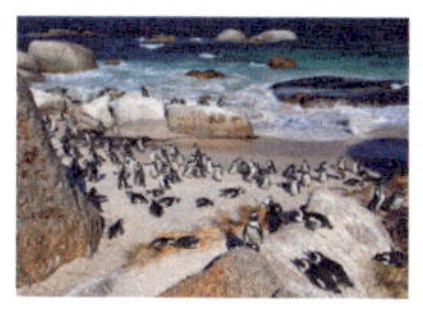

Stonewall Burk

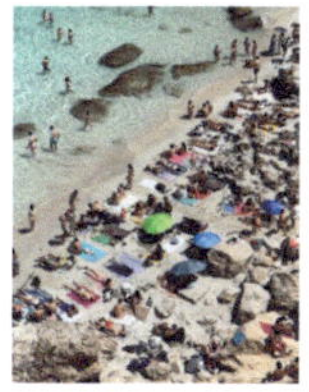

Altcada

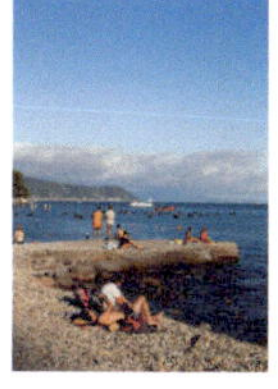

Kate Weybret

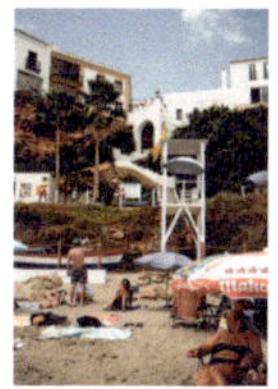

Nic Shuttleworth

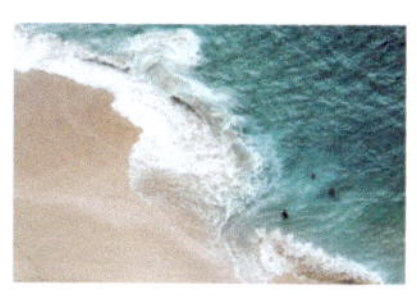

Austin Lansing

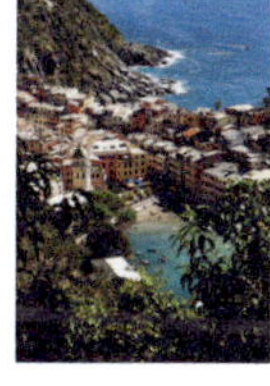

Kate Weybret

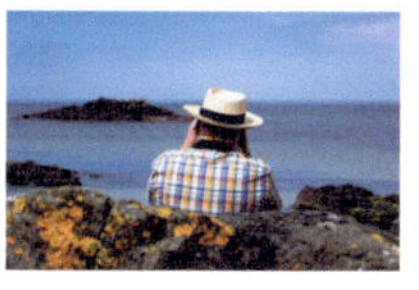

Ken J Rutherford

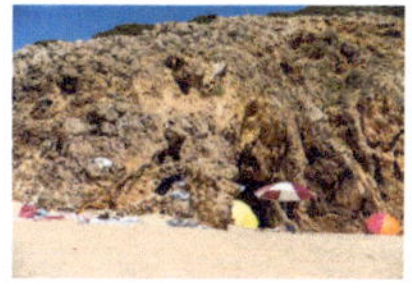

Becky Mursell

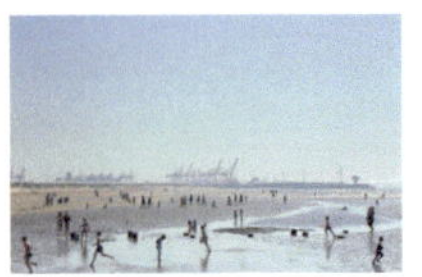
Brent Jones

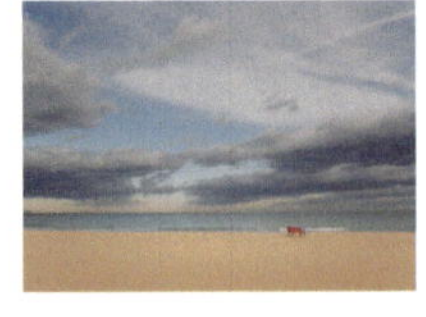
Terence Wright

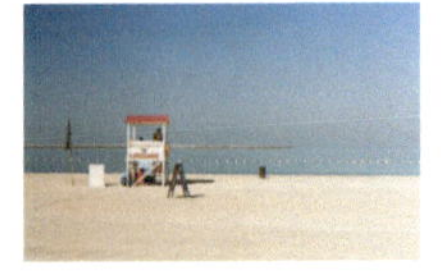
Fred Sansone

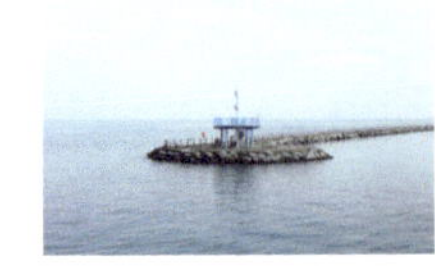
Tom Need

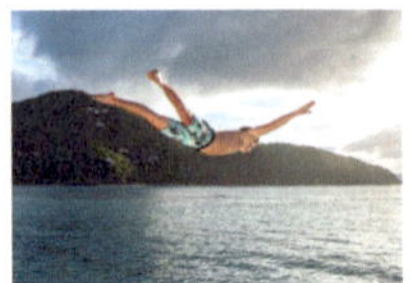
Molly O'Callaghan

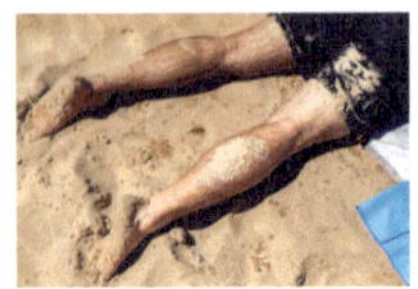
Becky Mursell

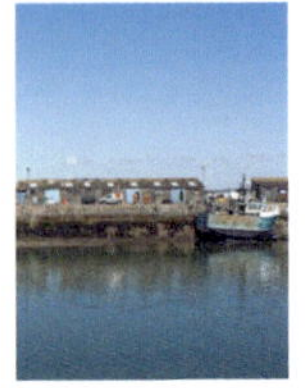
James Berrington

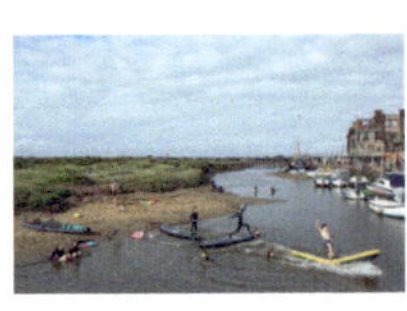
Brent Jones

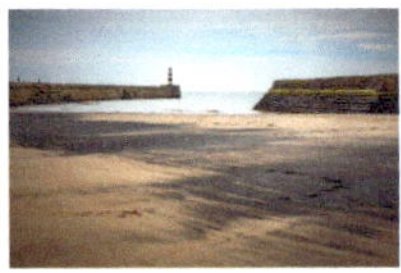
Dr Sam Welburn

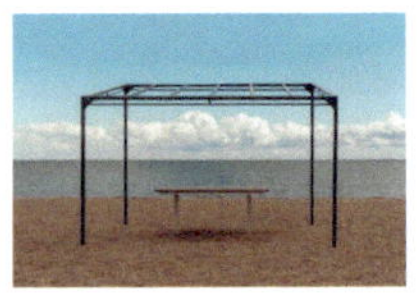
Dineke Versluis

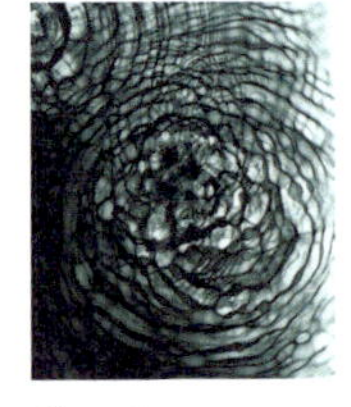
Sian Cann

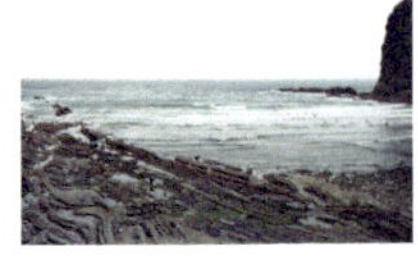
Jim Cooke

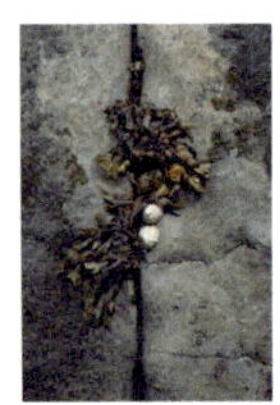
Sarah Deane

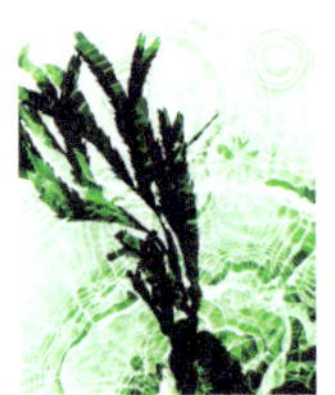
Sian Cann

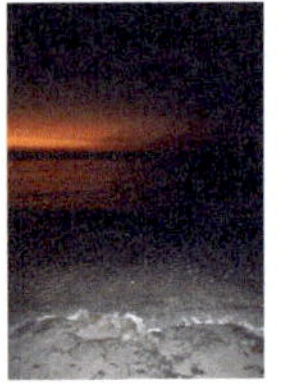
Jo Kalinowski

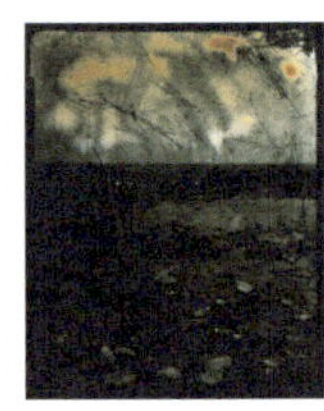
Ky Lewis

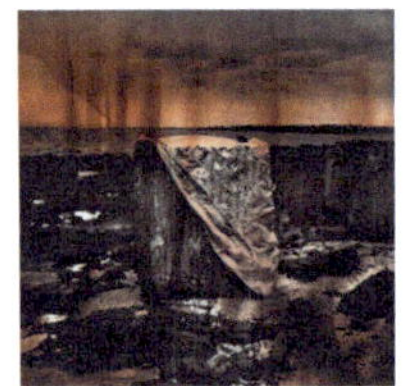
Wendy I Hardie

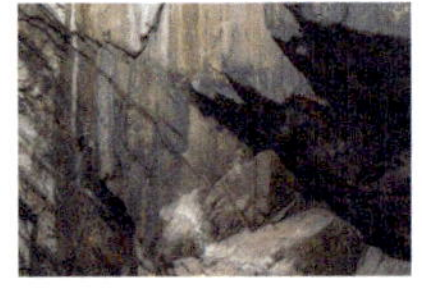
Anne Coveney

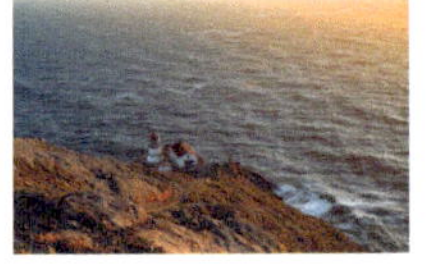
Vijay Sankar Anil

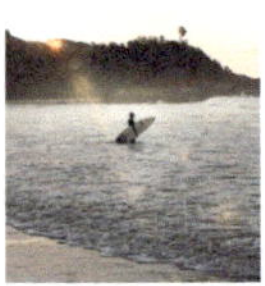
Mark Eden

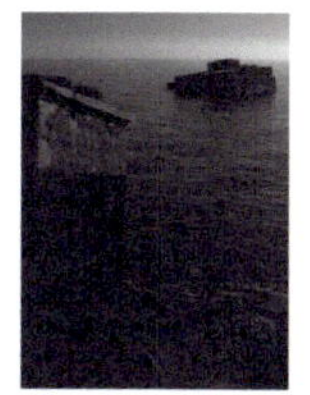
Alec Dent

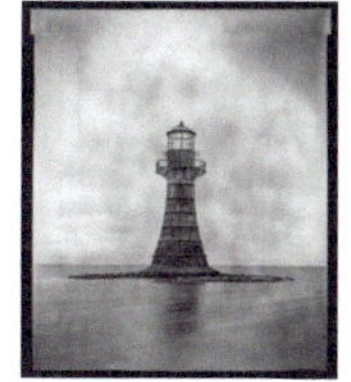
Peter Britton

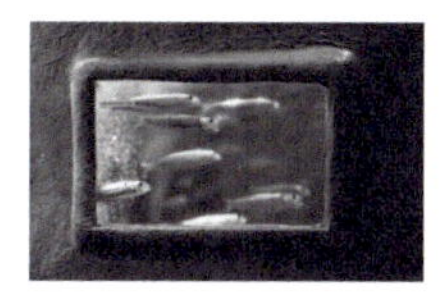
Martin Miklas

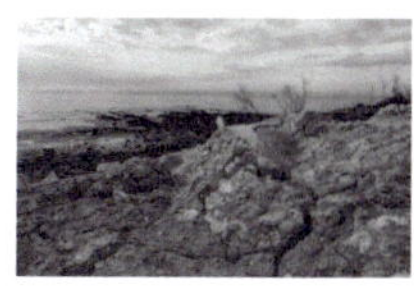
Matt E Lewis

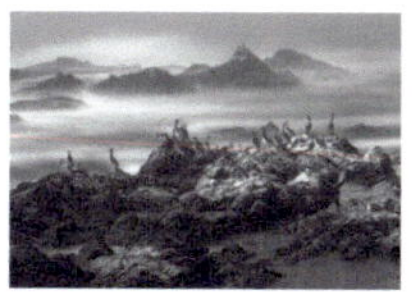
Phil Lewenthal

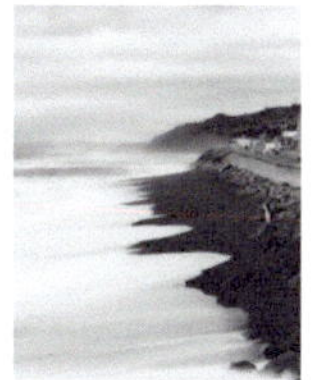
Alan Pelz-Sharpe

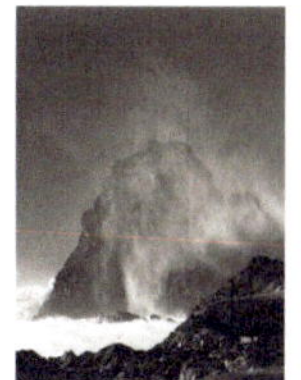
Austen Goldsmith

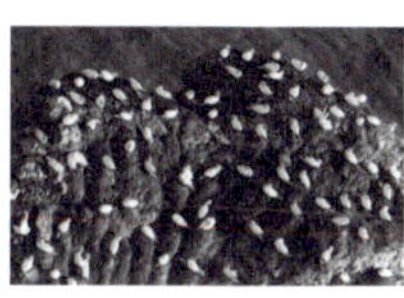
Stonewall Burk

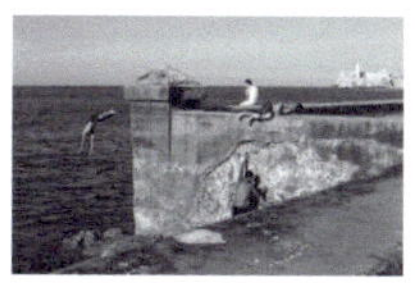
Zaklina Anderson

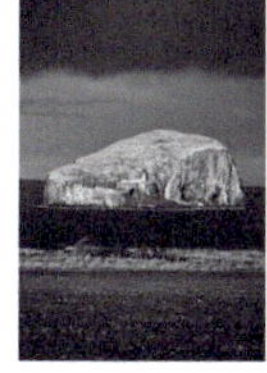
Mike Gorman

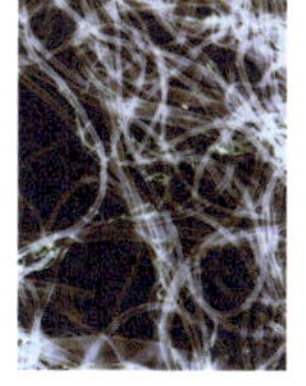
Anne Campbell

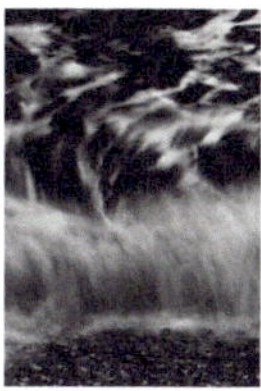
Jan Beesley

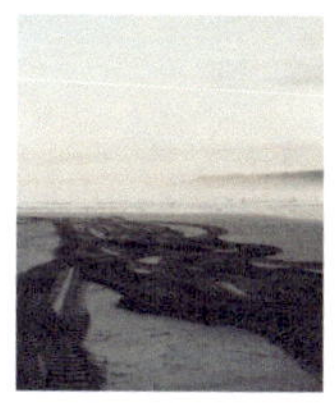
Janet Lees

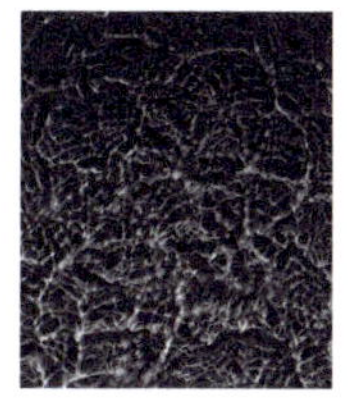
Sian Cann

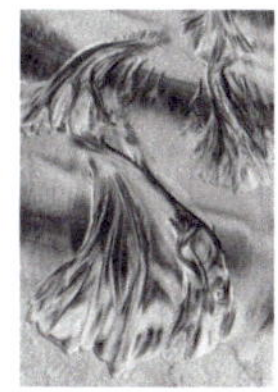
Loren Nelson

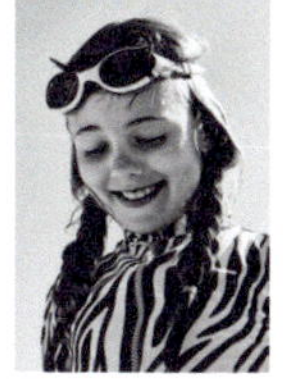
Nic Shuttleworth

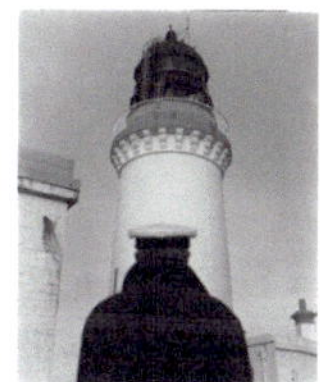
Conor Gault

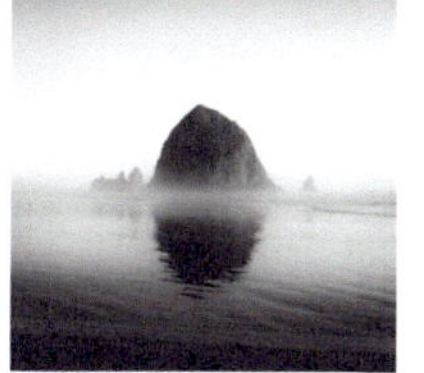
Kathryn Audet

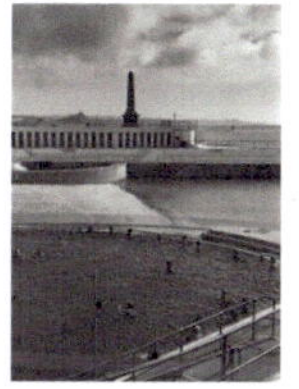
Austen Goldsmith

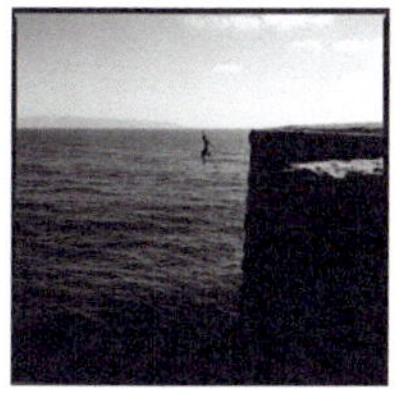
Alan Gignoux

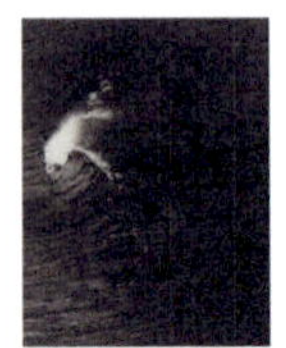

Ian Harrison

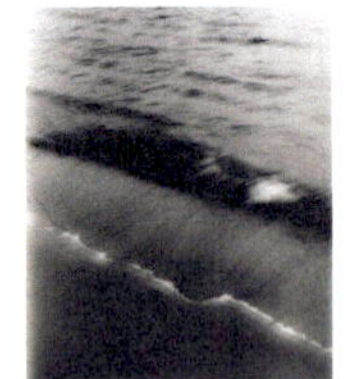

Tomas Zukovskij

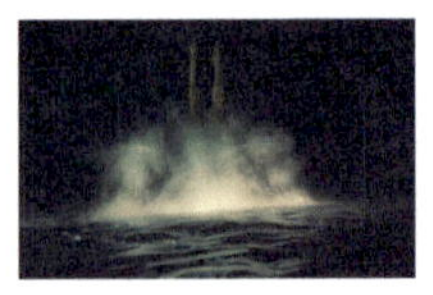

Claudia Rubner

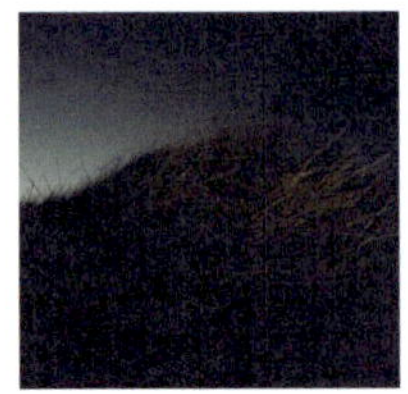

Grant Simon Rogers

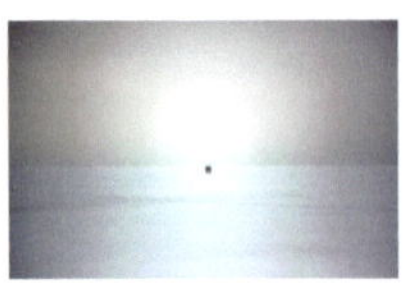

Mike Sutton

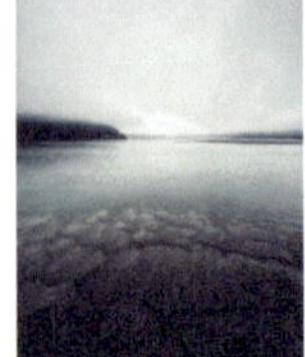

Janet Lees

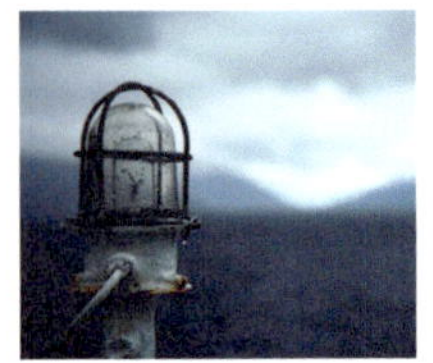

Nuala Mahon

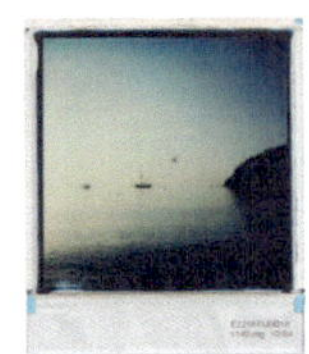

Kieran McPeake

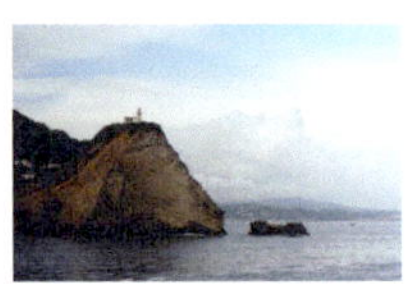

Fred Sansone

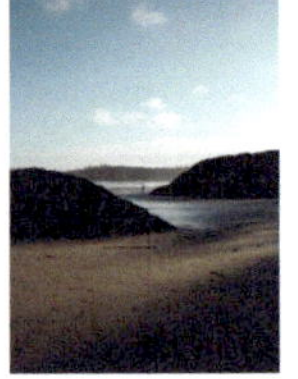

Tyler AW Burke

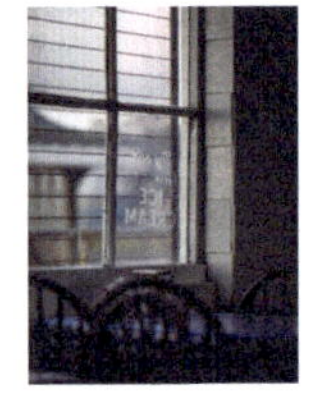

Nicola Parry

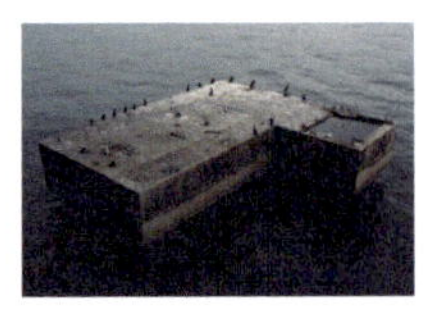

Tyler AW Burke

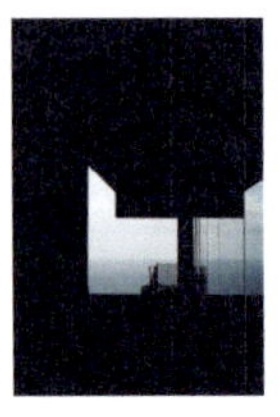

Ben Conley

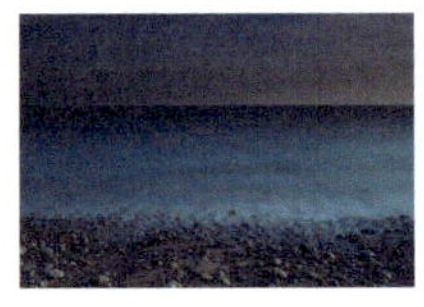

Nicholas Hodgson

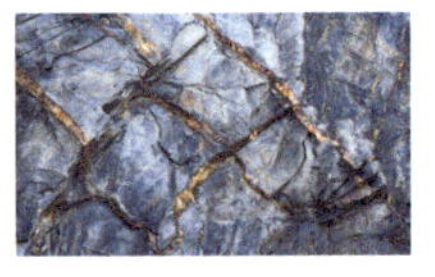

Kumudini Hajra

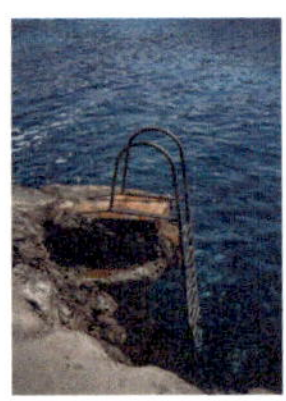

Gary Catlin

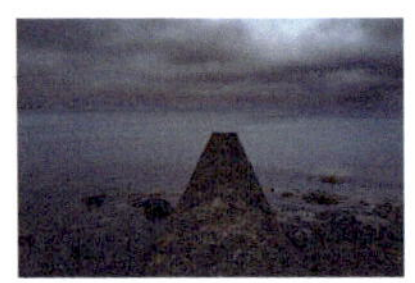

Geoff Duffield

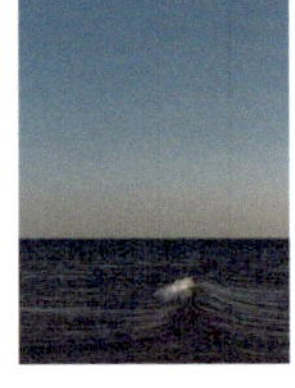

Dineke Versluis

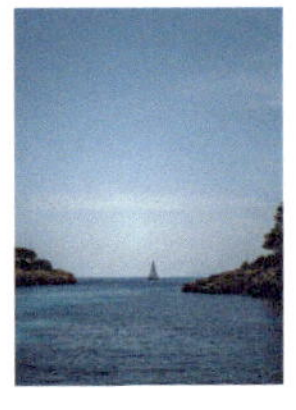

Gary Catlin

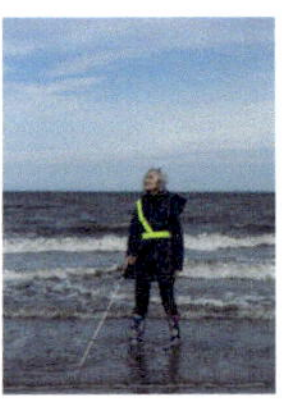

Rosita McKenzie

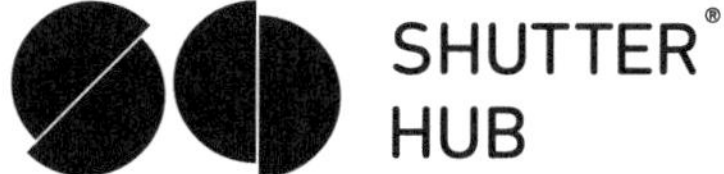

SHUTTER HUB EDITIONS is the publishing house from Shutter Hub, creating a collection of printed publications for people who love photography.

Shutter Hub is the UK based photography organisation providing opportunities, support and networking for creative photographers worldwide.

A supportive community for photographers, providing a platform for the development of ideas and careers.

SHUTTERHUB.ORG.UK

ISBN: 978-1-7399632-9-3
shutterhub.org.uk | @shutter_hub

shutterhub.org.uk/shutter-hub-editions-to-the-sea